THE ROAD TO OUR CABIN

BY

THOMAS F. HALL

*Dedicated to the memory of my brother, Dave Hall,
who first had the vision to own a family lake place
and took the leadership to make his vision happen.
The cabin has been a great blessing to our whole family.
Thank you doesn't go far enough.*

1968-1979

1979-present

Table of Contents

A SEED PLANTED

My father died when I was just fourteen years old. What an impact that had on our family of nine. Mom was left to raise me and my four younger brothers all by herself in our small house in south Minneapolis, Minnesota. My older sister, Gwen, was married and starting her own family. My older brother, Dave, married right after Dad died, so he left home also. They both did, however, stop back home often to check up on us boys and see how Mom was doing.

Mom was a wonderful cook and would always try to make our evening meals together a special time. Dave, Gwen, and Keith, Gwen's husband, joined us one evening as we all gathered around our large oak table in the dining room. We all were really looking forward to the fantastic meal Mom had prepared. Mom sat at the head of the table, and Gwen and Keith sat next to her. I (Tom) sat next to Keith, and my brothers Bob, Jon, Don, and Steve each took a chair. Dave sat at the far end of the table.

Dave was tall, strong, and very firm. None of us liked to cross Dave because if we did, we would come out on the losing end. Dave expected a lot of me after we lost Dad, and there was some conflict between us. He tried to take Dad's place in our lives, but we all struggled with Dave trying to be our father. Dave had a lot on his plate. He had worked at a steel firm for a while after graduating from high school but decided to change careers. Dave's wife, Marilyn, worked at a business office and supported him while he went to the University of Minnesota to get a degree in education.

After Mom blessed the food, we began to load our plates with roast beef, mashed potatoes, gravy, and vegetables.

"Pass the mashed potatoes!" yelled Jon as he finished his first helping.

Jon was eleven years old, short, strong, and a great athlete. He especially excelled in hockey. A confident, definite leader, Jon was outgoing with very few fears. He was the daredevil in our family and liked to live on the edge.

"Don't take so much that you won't eat it all," commented Bob.

Bob was two years older than Jon and wanted to make sure Jon ate everything on his plate. Bob was thirteen and two years younger than me. He was an excellent student and always wanted to do the right thing. He definitely knew how to stay out of trouble having watched my parents discipline me often. Bob was very dependable.

"Don't worry about it, Bob," muttered Jon with a sour look on his face as he secretly stuffed the crust from his bread under the edge of the table.

"My husband has something to say which just might be of interest to you outdoor fanatics," stated Gwen raising her voice slightly so we could all hear her.

Gwen was my only sister. She was smart, good looking, and loved her brothers. Gwen was seventeen when she married Keith, who was a year older than her. They had been married for a few years and had a young son named Scott. We boys often went to visit her and Keith after they got married. Gwen would cut our hair. She had taken over Dad's role in that area. We all loved Gwen!

"Gwen and I are going up to my parents' cabin next weekend," Keith said. "They won't be up there, so I asked them if I could invite the six wild Hall boys to join us. The cabin is on a small lake in northern Minnesota called Spirit Lake. It's just north of Mille Lacs and about a two hour drive away. We could swim, fish, have campfires, and just enjoy the outdoors."

"Tommy, we could catch lots of fish!" Steve said looking at me with his bright blue eyes.

Steve was the baby of the family. He was seven years old and my most impressionistic brother. He was cute and had a great smile with big dimples on his face. He and my brother, Don, hung out a lot together and shared the same friends. Steve loved life and wanted to be involved with everything us older brothers were doing. He loved action, activity, and all sports.

"Mom, we never ever go on a vacation. Do you think we could go to Keith's cabin?" I pleaded.

Mom gazed over at Dave without saying anything. She just had a puzzled expression on her face.

"Well," started Dave looking very serious, "I'm not doing anything next weekend and could drive. I can't take all the brothers in my car, Gwen, but if you and Keith could take the younger brothers in your car, I suppose it would work."

"Oh, Mom, let us go up to Keith's cabin! Please! Please!" chanted Don and Steve together.

Don was nine years old and, like Steve, was very excitable. Don was hard working and loved to work on projects with his neighborhood friends. He built a playhouse next to our house where his friends would come and hold secret meetings. Unfortunately, Don wasn't a good student and struggled with reading.

"Will it be safe up there by the lake?" questioned Mom. "I couldn't bear it if something happened to one of my boys."

"We'll keep a close eye on them, Mom. And if they go out in a boat, we'll make sure they wear life jackets," responded Gwen.

"Yes, Edla, we have enough life jackets for all your boys. They'll be safe. Won't they, Dave?" stated Keith with a serious look on his face.

This was rare because Keith usually had a sly smile and was always joking around.

"You don't have to worry about their safety, Mom. Between Keith, Gwen, and me they will be well supervised," responded Dave. "And, Tommy, you and your brothers don't go anywhere without my permission. Understood?"

"Understood, Dave," I answered and gazed at Jon with a gleam in my eye.

We all lit up. We could hardly believe we were going on a vacation to my brother-in law's cabin.

Things had been kind of rough for the Hall family over the past year. Our father, Glenn, had died suddenly of a massive heart attack. He just dropped dead in our living room. I wasn't home at the time, but Don had watched him fall. That was hard on Don. It was a difficult time for our whole family, but Mom took it the worst. My parents deeply loved and depended on one another. I think Mom was in shock for a couple of months and struggled with depression for over a year. I did worry about Mom and was glad when she got over her depression and became her old self again. She realized she had us five boys to live for and take care of.

At the time of my father's death, Dave was planning to get married the next month. That meant I would be the oldest of the brothers at home. I felt a huge burden to help Mom and keep my younger brothers in line. I didn't want that responsibility and wasn't very good at it. We all loved Mom, but we were undisciplined and hard to raise. Bob was the exception. He always obeyed Mom and tried to do the right thing all the time. I never worried about Bob. However, Jon, Don, and Steve were another story, and I was no angel myself.

We Hall boys eagerly waited for the day when our new adventure to Keith's cabin would begin. The day before the trip, my four younger brothers and I got together in our living room to discuss our plans.

"I have a rod and reel and a small tackle box which I will bring with me," I said to my brothers as we sat in a circle.

"I have a rod and reel too," added Bob. "It has a cork bobber and a small gold hook."

"We don't have any fishing rods," cried Jon as his lip began to quiver.

"Don't worry, little brothers. I talked to Gwen, and she told me there will be enough fishing gear for all of us," I said.

Jon stopped crying, and Steve and Don wiped the tears from their eyes as well.

"Bob, can you get a coffee can? We need to go into the backyard and dig for worms," I stated.

"Sure," answered Bob.

We dug a couple of dozen worms from Mom's garden. Bob filled the can with dirt and put a lid on top. Mom packed our suitcases that night. We could hardly wait.

The next day, Dave, Keith, and Gwen pulled in front of our two story, white, wooden house at about the same time. We were all waiting on the steps with our suitcases and fishing gear.

"Here they come!" yelled Don.

We jumped up and cheered as both cars parked in front of our house. We loaded up the cars, gave Mom a hug, and were off. Bob, Jon, and I rode with Dave. Steve and Don jumped into Keith's car. I sat in the front with Dave, and Jon and Bob sat in back.

"How long will it take to get there?" asked Jon.

"A little over two hours, but I don't want any of you bugging me about how long it will take to get there," stated Dave firmly as he tried to pick food out of his teeth with a wooden toothpick.

"We won't bug you, Dave," responded Bob in a serious voice.

"Shoot!" yelled Dave.

"What's the matter?" I questioned.

"I just broke this blasted toothpick off in my tooth. I'll need to go the dentist and have it drilled out!" he complained.

"That's too bad," I offered. "Maybe you can get another toothpick and pry it loose."

"I doubt that will work," he said. "It'll just have to stay there until we get home."

Halfway there, we stopped at a drive-in restaurant, ate hot-dogs, and drank root beers. After eating, we drove many miles on the highway and then turned onto a side road. That road became a dirt road.

"This must be the road that leads to Spirit Lake," commented Dave.

Sure enough, we soon saw a gorgeous lake on our left. We drove about another mile and followed Keith's car down a smaller road and into a driveway. We all jumped out of the car and stretched our legs. I gazed around and observed tall pine trees everywhere. There were also beautiful oak, maple, and birch trees.

"Is this what heaven is like, Lord?" I said pinching myself.

The air was crisp and clean. I took a deep breath and let the air slowly flow from my lungs. I gazed at my brothers. They were all wonder eyed as well.

In front of Keith's blue '56 Ford stood the cabin. It was made of long, narrow logs. It was a gray color and appeared weather beaten. A dock sat beyond the cabin extending out into the lake. Two boats were tied to it. The lake was gorgeous!

"This is it!" yelled Keith. "Get your things and come inside!"

We grabbed our stuff and walked into the cabin. It was just as beautiful on the inside as it was on the outside. The inside walls were logs as well with white material of some kind cemented between them. A stone fireplace stood at the far end of the cabin. Large front windows faced the lake giving us a fantastic view. A twelve point deer head was hanging on the living room wall along with some pictures and fishing rods. A stove, refrigerator, and a large wooden table with chairs sat in the kitchen. The smell of wood filled the air, and we could hear our steps as our shoes hit the wooden floor.

Keith took us three older boys into a bedroom with two bunk beds.

"This is where you will sleep while we're here," stated Keith.

We spread our sleeping bags on the bunks. I took the top bunk and Jon would sleep under me. Bob took the bottom bunk next to ours.

"Let's hit the sack, guys," stated Keith. "It's getting kind of late. I'll give you a tour tomorrow. Then, we can have some fun."

We undressed and slipped into our sleeping bags in our underwear. None of us boys slept in pajamas. We still don't.

The next morning we woke to smell the aroma of coffee, toast, bacon, and eggs filling the air. Keith had a scrumptious meal waiting for us to devour. We scrambled to the table, pulled up the chairs, and enjoyed our fantastic breakfast. When I was finished, I jumped up and headed for the door.

"Where are you going, little brother?" spoke Dave.

"Outside," I responded.

"Not until you do your chores," he responded.

"What chores?" I asked rather puzzled.

"Keith cooked us our breakfast, so we're going to clean up. Tom, you get to wash the dishes. Bob and Jon, you clear the table. Steve, you wipe the table. Don, you get to take out the garbage. No one leaves this cabin until all chores are done."

We all glanced at each other kind of shocked because Mom did all that work for us at home. But, we obeyed our brother. After we were finished cleaning up, Keith gave us a tour of his place. Just beyond his cabin was another cabin under construction made out of the same kind of logs.

"My family is building another cabin on our property to accommodate our growing family," Keith said. "As my siblings get older and have children, we are going to need more room."

During the daylight hours, the setting was even more impressive to me. As I stood in front of Keith's family's cabin, I realized it was built from natural logs that were notched at each end so they would fit perfectly on top of each other. My eyes scanned this structure with amazement. It was as if I had gone back in time and was observing a home in the wilderness in the 1800's. The cabin reminded me of a model home I had built out of Lincoln Logs.

"What are you staring at, Tommy?" questioned Keith as he stood beside me.

"This cabin! It's beautiful!"

"My family built it from scratch," Keith said. "The logs are from this property. We cut down the trees, peeled off the bark, and had the logs cured at the local lumberyard."

"How did you know what to do?"

"We didn't really know how until we read some books and asked a lot of questions."

"It turned out fantastic! I love it here already," I replied.

I turned my attention to the lake. Keith's family had purchased two lots on Spirit Lake. They were wooded and high off the lake. The view was magnificent. I observed how the tree line around the lake was punctuated by small cabins. Keith's lot had wooden steps cut into the hill leading down to the crystal blue water.

"Tommy, get your rod and reel," Jon yelled. "Let's go fishing!"

"Well, I guess it's time to go fishing," Keith replied with a grin on his face.

I rushed to Dave's car, grabbed my rod and reel and the can of worms, and sprinted down the stairs. My brothers were all anxiously waiting. They had their life jackets on and their fishing gear in hand. They were ready to board the boats. Keith had two boats tied to the dock with 7 horse Johnson motors on them.

"Dave, you load up the first boat with Don and Tom. I'll take Bob, Jon, and Steve with me," Keith said.

"Where is a good spot to catch sunnies?" yelled Dave as he pulled the starting rope and the motor roared to life.

"Just around that first point," shouted Keith pointing his finger towards the north part of the lake. "There's a brown cabin high above the lake which you'll see as you round the bend. About twenty yards past the cabin is a twenty-five foot hole that's loaded with sunfish."

Dave accelerated the boat by turning the throttle handle on the motor. We pulled the boat around the point and spotted the brown cabin. Dave shut the motor off about twenty feet past the cabin and thirty feet from shore.

"This looks like the hole Keith was talking about," Dave said as he dropped the anchor.

Don was sitting in front, I was in the middle, and Dave sat in the back of the boat. I handed a worm to Dave. I broke another worm in half, handed one half to Don, and began to place my half on my hook. I had done a lot of fishing off the public dock at Lake Nokomis near our home in the city, so I knew what I was doing.

"I don't know how to put the worm on the hook, Tommy," complained Don.

"I'll show you, little brother. After that, you'll have to bait your own hook," I ordered.

I grabbed his hook, threaded the worm through the point, and jabbed its slippery body through several times until it was secure.

"The fish will really have to work at it to strip this bait off," I said.

I took Don's rod and cast it into the water about ten feet from the boat. The red and white bobber floated on top of the water while the lead sinker dropped down with the worm dangling on the hook.

"Watch your bobber, Don. When it goes under the water, give your rod a jerk to set the hook in the fish's mouth," I instructed.

Before I could finish my own hook, his bobber began bouncing up and down.

"Look at my bobber!" whispered Don excitedly.

"Wait patiently. When it goes completely under the water, set the hook," I responded.

The bobber went up and down several times before it finally disappeared under the water.

"Now!" I yelled.

Don jerked his rod, and it began to bend at the top.

"I got one! I got one!" screamed Don.

The fish dove from one side to another. Don was reeling way too fast.

"Slow down, Don!" yelled Dave. "Play the fish out and let the drag work."

Finally, Don got the fish close, and I jerked it into the boat. It was a nice sunny just a little bigger than the size of my hand.

"Tommy, I got a big one! Look at my rod bend!" Dave screamed suddenly.

He did not listen to his own advice and reeled as hard as he could. His rod was bent over, and he was cranking hard. Finally, the fish flew out of the water and into the boat. It was just a little sunfish.

"Some fish you caught there, Dave," I joked.

"That's not funny, Tommy! It felt huge. How could a little fish like that bend my rod and pull so hard?"

We discussed the situation and came to the conclusion that a northern or other larger fish must have had the sunny in its mouth. Then, when Dave pulled with all his might, the larger fish opened its mouth and the little sunny flew into the boat. It was hysterical to watch my older brother pull so hard and only be rewarded with a small little sunny.

This day was a day I will never forget. The sky was a clear blue, and the warmth of the sun rays splashed on my face. A cool breeze ruffled my hair. I breathed deeply as the oxygen filled and cooled my lungs. I was with my brothers, catching fish, surrounded by water, trees, and wilderness.

"How could heaven be any better than this?" I wondered.

Just as I was basking in my own dream world of tranquility, Don stood up to cast his line into the water. Instead of hanging on to the rod, Don opened his hand, and his whole rod and reel went flying into the lake. He stood dumbfounded as it slowly sank to the bottom. Don's face turned red, and he began to cry. Dave went nuts.

"Don!" he screamed. "That was not our rod and reel. It belonged to Keith's family. You'll have to dive to the bottom of the lake and retrieve it."

"I can't, Dave. It's too deep, and I can't swim that good," whined Don.

Dave went on and on angrily yelling at Don. I felt bad that this beautiful experience was seemingly ruined because of this negative experience.

"Don can't swim for that rod, Dave," I finally said. "It's way too deep. It was an accident, Dave. We'll just have to pay for the fishing rod."

"Do you have any money, Tommy?" Dave snapped back.

"No, I don't! We'll just have to work and save our money until we can pay for it," I stated matter-of-factly.

Dave finally settled down, and we went back to Keith's cabin. We had caught about twenty sunnies and had them in a bucket of water. Keith and my other brothers returned to the dock at about the same time. They held up a stringer with about six fish on it. There were a couple of nice sized walleyes, a couple of bass, and a northern.

Dave talked privately to Keith about the rod incident. We decided to pool our money to pay for the lost rod. Don felt really bad. I told him it was an accident and wasn't the end of the world. He finally settled down.

Keith took all the fish and showed us how to clean them. After the fish were all cleaned, he buried the fish guts in the woods. For lunch, we had fresh fish with diced potatoes. It was delicious! That afternoon, we swam in the fresh clean water of Spirit Lake and went on a boat ride around the lake.

After supper, Keith built a campfire. The sun was setting on the horizon, and the aroma of the wood fire filled the air. We roasted marshmallows and made s'mores. S'mores are roasted marshmallows and a piece of Hershey chocolate pressed between two graham crackers. They were delicious. Keith told some ghost stories, we sang some songs, and we reflected on moments from our day. For my brothers and me, this trip to Keith's parents' cabin was a lifetime memory. Seeds were planted in all our hearts. We had never had an experience like this in all our lives.

A DREAM CONCEIVED

"Tommy, I would like to share a dream with you," Dave offered as he walked into our home one summer day.

"What is it, Dave?" I questioned with my eyes wide open wondering what my big brother was thinking.

"Let's go for a walk and talk for a while, so I can brainstorm with you."

We ambled out of the house and began strolling toward Sibley Park, which was right down the street. Dave was the firstborn in our family of seven siblings. He was the leader of us kids, and we all looked up to him. At the time of this conversation, Dave was married, and I was fifteen years old. Bob was thirteen, Jon was eleven, Don was nine, and Steve was seven. Evidently, Dave's dream concerned all of my brothers.

"I want to fulfill Dad's dream of having a lake home," Dave shared.

"Fat chance," I thought to myself because we were living just one step above the poverty level. Putting food on the table was a real issue for our family.

"How could we ever afford to buy a lake home, Dave?" I responded.

"We could begin by saving money."

"What money?" I questioned.

We found ourselves sitting on a bench at Sibley Park.

"We could start a bank account," Dave suggested. "I would put in five dollars per week, and you could give me a dollar. We could ask Bob and Jon to put in fifty cents a week, and Don and Steve could put in twenty-five cents."

I stared into Dave's eyes to see if he was just humoring me. The look he gave back was dead serious.

"Dave, it would take us forever to save enough money at that rate."

"No, it wouldn't, Tommy. We would have close to four hundred dollars the first year. As you boys got older, we could increase the contributions. You could come up with a dollar a week, couldn't you?"

"Sure. I caddie in the summer and could do some odd jobs around the neighborhood during the school year. I'm sure a dollar a week wouldn't be too difficult to come up with."

"What do you think, Tommy? Do you want to give it a shot?" Dave questioned.

"Where would we keep the money?"

"You have that little box in your room. We would all put in our contributions each week. Then, I would pick up the money when I'm able to stop by and put it in a bank account. I need you to talk to your brothers and get a commitment from them. They have to be serious about it or else it won't work. Each one of us has to place his contribution in the box each week."

"A lake home for the Hall boys. Just maybe, it might work," I remarked as we got up from the bench and walked toward home.

As Dave drove away in his blue, torpedo back Chevy, I stood and pondered for a while. Sitting down on our front steps, I tried to visualize us having a home on a beautiful lake somewhere in northern Minnesota, the Land of 10,000 Lakes. It seemed like an impossible dream.

That evening after supper, I gathered my brothers outside of our house. I had them sit on the back steps, and I faced them.

"I have a little proposition that I would like to suggest to you, little brothers," I stated.

"Are we going to play a neighborhood game?" asked Jon.

"No, it's a little more serious than that."

"What's the matter, Tommy?" questioned Bob.

"Nothing's really the matter. How would you guys like to be part of a project that could affect our entire lives?" I continued.

My four brothers stared at me in bewilderment.

"I had a long talk with Dave today, and this concerns all of us."

"What did you and Dave talk about, Tommy?" asked Steve.

"Well, to tell you the truth, I thought he was kidding me at first. But, when I looked into his eyes, I knew he was serious."

"What is it, Tommy? You're killing us," responded Jon.

"He shared a dream with me that's for all of us. However, it will take a huge commitment from all of us if we are going to pull this thing off."

"What thing, Tommy?" questioned Don.

"Dave wants us to have a lake home some day, and he thinks we can pull it off. He will provide the leadership, but we all have to do our part."

"What's our part, Tommy?" asked Bob.

"Well, it takes money to have a lake home. Right?"

"Right!" they all responded in unison.

"That means we will have to save on a regular basis. Dave suggested we start a lake fund. He would put in five dollars a week. I would put in a dollar, Bob and Jon would put in fifty cents, and Don and Steve would put in twenty-five cents every week. We would all have to earn our own money because Mom doesn't have money to give us. Do you think you could all come up with that amount every week? If you can't, Dave said we shouldn't even think about this idea."

I just stared into their eyes while this idea sank into their minds. After a few minutes, Bob spoke up.

"Tommy, I think it's a great idea. I can come up with fifty cents a week, but that's not very much for a lake home. It would take us forever!"

"That's what I thought too, Bob. It might take a few years, but as we get older, we can each add a little more to the pot. Pretty soon, we'd all match Dave's contribution of five dollars per week. It would add up sooner than you think."

"Where are we going to get the money?" asked Steve.

"Is there anything you can do to earn twenty-five cents a week?" I asked looking directly into his bright blue eyes.

"We could all help each other. We could do jobs for our neighbors like raking leaves, cutting grass, or taking their dogs for a walk," declared Bob.

"The thing is that we can't miss a payment at any time. You know how strict Dave is. If any one of us misses, he will cancel the whole idea," I stated in a very serious tone.

"Let's go for it, Tommy. I would love a lake home because I love to fish," stated Jon.

"Me too!" shouted Don.

"I have a little box in my room on my dresser. That's where we'll put the money each week. If any one of us can't come up with the money, we'll help each other. Once the money is in the box, no one, and I mean no one, takes any money out. Understood?"

"Understood, Tom," they all said together.

So every Friday night, Dave would drop by our house after work, pick up the money from the box in my bedroom, and put the money in a bank account he had started. We all managed to put in our money each week without any trouble. After four years of saving, Dave announced that we had enough money in the savings account to soon begin looking for a lake lot. I had graduated from high school and was working at Donaldson's Warehouse, so I was matching Dave's amount of five dollars per week. Dave was very busy teaching school and coaching hockey, so he didn't come over as often. The money in the box would build up until he could come by to take it all to the bank.

One Saturday, I was playing golf at Hiawatha Golf Course with a friend of mine. He had a nice set of Wilson Staff golf clubs which he let me hit from time to time. I really loved those golf clubs. After we finished playing eighteen holes of golf, we went into the building, bought cokes, and sat at one of the tables.

"Tom, how do you like my clubs?" asked my friend, Bob.

"They're great clubs, Bob."

"How would you like to buy them?" questioned Bob.

"I really can't afford any clubs right now," I responded.

"I'm going to buy a new set this weekend, and I'll give you a great deal on this set if you are interested."

"How much do you want for them?" I asked.

"Eighty dollars."

"That's a great price," I answered. "Can I pay you next weekend when I get my check?"

"No! If you want to buy them at this price, you'll have to pay for them today."

"Let me think about it, and I'll call you tonight, Bob," I responded.

As I walked to my car, my mind was filled with thoughts of how I could get my hands on eighty dollars to buy those clubs. It was a good deal, and I greatly wanted to have those clubs.

When I arrived home, I ran upstairs to my bedroom. I opened the box where we put in the money for our cabin, pulled out the bills, and counted eighty-seven dollars. Dave hadn't been by to pick up the money for a while. I thought I could take out eighty dollars and pay the money back when I received my check the next Saturday. No one would know the difference. So, I took the money out of the box, drove over to Bob's house, and purchased the Wilson Staff golf clubs.

On Friday night, Dave stopped by to check the box. He went upstairs to my room expecting to see close to one hundred dollars. Instead, he found only seven dollars. He came roaring downstairs with fire in his eyes. We were all sitting in the living room.

"Who took money out of the box?" he yelled.

We all just look at one another dumbfounded.

"Someone took money out of the box, and I want to know who it was," he screamed.

"I took the money, Dave," I mumbled.

"Where is it, Tommy?" he shouted as he stared daggers at me.

"I don't have it. I spent it on a set of golf clubs," I admitted.

"You did what?" he shouted.

"I get paid on Saturday, Dave. I'll give you the money tomorrow."

"That's no good! The deal is off! I'll go to the bank, get all the money, and we'll divide it up according to how much we put in," stated Dave firmly.

"Tommy, why did you take the money? You said we should never take money out of the box once we put it in," moaned Bob with tears in his eyes.

"Yeah, Tommy! I really wanted to have this cabin, and you screwed it up," cried Jon.

Everyone was crying and upset with me. I knew I had to do something quick. I looked at Dave. He was so upset that he could hardly talk.

"Tommy, if we are going to own a cabin together, then we need to trust one another. You just broke my trust. I don't want this cabin if I can't trust you. The deal is off. I'm sorry, Tommy, but you just blew it for all of us. Thanks a lot!" Dave shouted.

"Dave, please! I get paid tomorrow, and my check will be for one hundred and ten dollars. You can have it all. I want this cabin. I want to own it with all my brothers. It was Dad's dream to own a cabin with his family. We are so close. We can do it now. Please, Dave, forgive me! I wanted those clubs so bad. I didn't think you would come by tonight. The money would have been there tomorrow. I was wrong. Please don't ruin the dream because of me. I couldn't live with that," I pleaded.

Dave listened, and his eyes began to soften.

"Tommy, once the money is in the box, it stays there until I pick it up and take it to the bank. Do you think just because you want something for yourself, you can take our money and use it for selfish purposes?"

"No, I don't! I'm sorry. I was wrong. It will never happen again. I will never touch the money in that box again," I stated emphatically.

Dave stared at my little brothers.

"Do you all realize how close Tommy came to spoiling our dream?" Dave said firmly. "We are investing in something that we could have for the rest of our lives. It could be something that will hold our family together. I'm going to give Tommy another chance, but I want you brothers to know that we need to trust each other. Tommy broke our trust. If it happens again, it is all over with no questions asked."

It was an emotional time for all of us. I had almost ruined our dream. We had been saving our money for four years and had close to one thousand dollars in the bank. We were about to begin shopping for some lakeshore property. Dave was right to come down hard on me, and I would never make that mistake again. He could trust me with all the money in the world, and I would never touch it again. I was grateful for a second chance.

When Dave left our house, I just stared at Bob, Jon, Don, and Steve.

"I'm so sorry, guys!" I stated with tears rolling down my cheeks. "I almost blew it for all of us. I guess this is more serious than I thought! When I thought our dream might be over because of my selfishness, it really hit me. I love you guys! I want this dream to come true. I will never do anything to destroy this dream of ours again. Who would have ever thought the Hall brothers could have a lake home? It's going to happen, and I'm going to do everything in my power to make sure it does!"

OUR SEARCH FOR LAND

One spring day in 1963, I was peering out our front window. I noticed Dave's yellow station wagon pulling up to our house. Dave walked into the living room.

"Tommy, where are your brothers?"

"Bob and Jon are here, but I'm not sure where the younger ones are."

"Get Bob and Jon down here. I've got some news I want to share with you guys," Dave declared.

I went upstairs and found Bob and Jon in their rooms.

"Hey, guys, Dave is here and wants to talk to us in the living room."

The three of us hustled down the stairs and saw Dave sitting on the couch waiting for us.

"Sit down, little brothers. I've got some news."

I sat in our big easy chair while Jon and Bob plopped down on the carpet.

"What is it?" questioned Bob with a curious expression on his face.

"I just deposited some money into our bank account and realized we have enough money to search for some land to build our cabin."

Our eyes lit up, and our expressions radiated our joy. We gave Dave our undivided attention.

"We have one thousand dollars in the bank, and I've done some checking on the price of lake lots. I've checked in northern Minnesota around the Brainerd area, but the property up there is way too expensive."

"Does that mean we will have to wait and save more money?" I asked.

"No, it just means that lakeshore property is just too expensive in Minnesota. So, I called some realtors in Wisconsin and made an appointment this weekend to look at some spots over there."

"Are there any good lakes in Wisconsin?" asked Jon with a disappointed look on his face.

"Actually, I think the lakes in Wisconsin are even better than the ones here. The ones we are going to look at are closer to Minneapolis too. I've made an appointment with a realtor in Spooner, Wisconsin, which is just a little over a hundred miles away, for this weekend."

"I've never heard of Spooner, Dave," I said.

"It's a nice sized town just about fifty miles from Taylor Falls. I told Marilyn we will be searching for lakeshore property this weekend. I'll be here at 8:00 AM sharp to pick you all up. I want all the brothers to be dressed and ready to go, Tommy. Is that clear?"

"Yes, Sir! We not only will be ready, but we'll be sitting on the steps waiting for you. You can take that to the bank!" I stated with a huge grin on my face.

Jon and Bob were grinning from ear to ear as well.

"I'll bring the checkbook. If we find what we want, we'll pay cash for it," stated Dave with a confident expression on his face.

"This is too good to be true! The Hall boys are going to search for lakeshore property and pay cash for it," I declared with amazement.

"We've all worked hard to save this money! Now, it's time to get some land and make our dream, Dad's dream, come true!" explained Dave seriously.

"Jon, we are going to build a cabin, go fishing and swimming, and have a place to escape to!" I yelled.

"Are you serious, Dave? Do you think we really have enough money to buy a lot?" questioned Bob.

"Yup. I've got to get home now, but I'll be back bright and early Saturday morning," responded Dave as he headed for the door.

As the back door slammed, we just sat and stared at one another for a minute or two.

"Can you believe it?" said Bob. "We are going to buy some lakeshore property."

That evening around the dinner table, I told the big news to Mom.

"Dave is picking us up on Saturday morning to search for some lake property in Wisconsin."

"I know you boys have been saving money, but do you have enough to buy a lot?" questioned Mom with a serious expression on her face.

"Dave said we have enough," Jon piped in.

"Mom, can you set the alarm for 6:30 AM on Saturday? We need to get up early, get dressed, and finish breakfast before Dave gets here. I told him we would all be sitting on the steps waiting when he drove up," I replied.

Before Mom could say anything, Bob broke in.

"Mom, could you make us each a lunch? We all love tuna fish sandwiches."

"Yes, boys, I'll wake you up at 6:30 AM. We'll have cereal, and there will be lunches for everyone, including Dave," responded Mom with a huge grin. "You boys are going to fulfill your father's dream. I am so proud of all of you!"

When Dave pulled up to the curb on Saturday morning, we were all waiting on the steps holding our bag lunches. After piling into Dave's car, we headed for Wisconsin. We drove up Highway 8 and headed for Taylors Falls. We knew where that was because Dad had taken us there once before. We had climbed the rocks and spent a wonderful day exploring the banks of the St. Croix River. When we reached Taylors Falls, we crossed the bridge over the St. Croix River. We were welcomed by a sign shaped like Wisconsin with the state's name engraved on it.

"It didn't take us long to get to Wisconsin," yelled Steve.

"It looks a little hillier than Minnesota," Bob noticed.

"I actually believe Wisconsin is more beautiful than Minnesota," Dave stated. "We're going to explore some incredible lakes today. Are you guys ready for this?"

"Yes!" we all screamed at the same time.

As we drove through the hilly country, we observed clear blue lakes, thick forests, and numerous dairy farms with red barns and huge silos. It was springtime, and the fields were freshly plowed. No crops had popped out of the ground yet.

"What kind of cows are those with black and white spots?" questioned Steve.

"Those are Holsteins," stated Bob.

"How do you know that?" asked Don.

"They look just like the cows in Goodhue, Minnesota, where Mom used to live. Remember when Dad drove us to the farm and we saw all those black and white cows?" asked Bobby.

"Yes!" responded Jon. "We got to watch our uncle milk the cows. He even shot some milk at the kitty who was watching him."

We all laughed at the way Jon explained it.

My five brothers and I were headed to a place to purchase some lakeshore property. We had no idea what we were looking for or how all this was going to happen. We trusted our big brother, Dave, who was leading us on this mission he had organized. The outcome was completely unknown to us, and it almost seemed like an impossible mission. However, we all knew the final outcome would be something really special.

When we pulled into the town of Spooner, we found the real estate office. We got out of the car and walked into the front of the small building. A receptionist sat at the front desk.

"Hi, my name is Dave Hall. I have an appointment to see a real estate agent at 10:30 AM," Dave stated.

I looked at the clock on the wall. We were five minutes late.

"I will see if John is ready to see you. He has been expecting you this morning," she replied as she sized up us six boys with a look of wonder on her face.

The young woman disappeared into an office and soon emerged with a smile on her face.

"John will be out in just a minute," she said as she returned to her desk.

John walked out of his office. He was a short man in his late forties with black hair that was slightly gray at the temples. He wore a blue suit, had glasses on, and looked friendly with a grin on his face.

"You must be Dave," he said to my brother. "I've been expecting you. Who are all these young men with you?"

"These are my brothers, Tom, Bob, Jon, Don, and Steve."

We each shook his hand as he smiled and gazed directly into our eyes.

"So, you boys are looking for some lakeshore property. I've got three spots picked out for you that you might be interested in," stated John.

"Can we look at the properties?" asked Dave.

"Sure! That's what I had in mind. I'll drive my car out to the sites, and you can follow me in your car. The best way to purchase property is to see it first hand."

We followed John to the first site, which was about ten miles from Spooner on Trego Lake. We drove down a dirt road and turned into the lot. It was about eight hundred feet deep and was filled with trees. It had one hundred feet of lakeshore. We jumped out of the car and walked to the edge of a hill overlooking the lake. It was a wonderful sight. The sky was clear blue, and the sun shone brightly in the morning sky. The water was a darker blue, and trees lined the far side of the lake. As I turned to survey the lot, I noticed several varieties of trees. There were tall white and red pines in front with a scattering of maple, oak, and birch trees throughout the lot. I've always loved trees and studied them in school. I could identify most of the trees in Minnesota.

I took a deep breath and let the clean fresh air cool my lungs. The brush was thick, but I tried to visualize a cabin sitting on this lot. My brothers seemed to be doing the same. They were turning around and trying to take everything in.

"How do you boys like this site?" asked John directing his question to Dave.

"It's a beautiful setting, but I noticed an inlet coming into the lake on one side and going out the other," Dave answered.

"Actually, Trego Lake is a widening of the river. It would be great to be on this lake because it feeds into two other lakes," stated John.

"How much does this lot sell for?" questioned Dave.

"This lot sells for two thousand eight hundred dollars," responded John.

Dave gazed in my direction as if to say "It's too expensive for us, Tom."

We all loved the setting, but Dave asked John to take us to the other two sites. The next lot John showed us was located in Washington County on Ellsworth Lake. This lot was highly elevated off the lake with a fantastic view. Ellsworth Lake was a much smaller lake than Trego, but once again the setting was gorgeous.

"Jon, let's go down to the water!" I yelled.

We found a small path leading to the shore-line and scampered down the hill. The water was clear, but there were weeds and bull rushes sticking up from the sandy bottom. I picked up a stone, threw it across the water, and watched it skip five times.

"Wow, Tommy, that was pretty good!" shouted Steve as he picked up a stone and tried to beat my throw.

We all took turns throwing stones in the water while Dave and John were talking on the land above us.

"Everybody up here!" Dave yelled after a few minutes.

We all scampered up the path, and Dave told us to get into the car.

"This lot is too high off the lake, and the lake is too small," Dave said as we drove off. "John is going to show us Rooney Lake."

"How much do they want for this lot, Dave?" I asked.

"Two thousand dollars," Dave responded.

As we drove to Rooney Lake, we questioned Dave about what we were looking for.

"We want a good size lake that has some depth to it. I want it to be good for fishing and swimming. And, we're looking for a lot that costs about one thousand dollars," Dave commented.

We surveyed two more lakes before heading back to the real estate office with John. When we arrived back in Spooner, we went into the office. Dave told John that we were most interested in the lot on Trego Lake, but we needed to discuss it further. He said he would give him a call and let him know our decision next week. Dave and John shook hands, and we all climbed back into the car.

As we were driving home, Dave told us that he wasn't interested in any of the lots John had showed us.

"How come?" I questioned.

"The lots and lakes were all very nice, but they were either too high off the water, the lake was too small, or the price was too high."

"Will we ever find a place?" whined Don.

"Yes, Don," stated Dave. "We'll come back next week and check with Lakes Real Estate in Siren. I've already made an appointment."

The next Saturday, we drove back to Wisconsin and visited the Lakes Real Estate office in Siren. A gentleman by the name of Fred drove us to several sites. None of them worked for us. As we were driving back to Siren on County Road A, we noticed an incredible lake to our left.

We pulled off the road at a restaurant and bar located right on the lake called "The Sand Bar". We went inside and ordered hamburgers and french fries. As we ate our food, we stared out a big picture window at the beautiful clear blue water of North Sand Lake. The sight made for a magnificent view.

Dave was sitting next to Fred and drinking a root beer when he asked, "Are there any lots for sale on this lake?"

"As a matter-of-fact, a road just opened on a peninsula," stated Fred. "Would you like to see the lots? They are just up the road from here."

"Absolutely!" responded Dave.

After we finished lunch, we drove a little further down County Road A and took a left onto Leef Road. We drove about a mile and a half and turned left onto a dirt road which was labeled Peninsula Road. The woods were so thick we couldn't even see the sky. We noticed water on both sides of the road. When we got to the bottom of a small hill, Fred stopped his car in front of ours. I hopped out of the car and stared up the hill. A huge oak tree stood in the middle of the road. The road split and went around the tree on both sides.

"That is the biggest oak tree I've ever seen. It must be too big to bring down," I said to Jon.

"We are on a peninsula, so there is water on both sides," Fred stated. "The lots on the left are on the big side of the lake."

Most of the trees had been cut down on those lots. Bare sandy lots with a few trees standing in the front and back were all that was left. A huge pile of logs in the back of the lot indicated the amount of trees that had been removed. I didn't like that.

We left the car on the road and walked down to the lakeshore. There was a beautiful sand beach. The water was crystal clear, and the bottom was totally sandy with no weeds or vegetation. It looked like a natural swimming beach. The lot was about two hundred feet deep and just slightly elevated from the water. Everything was perfect except there were hardly any trees. I thought this lot could work for us, but I knew we would have to plant a lot of trees.

"How much is this lot selling for?" asked Dave.

"This is going for two thousand five hundred dollars," responded Fred.

Fred must have noticed Dave's eyes drop, so he continued talking.

"This is a prime lake. It is clear and deep, has a sandy bottom, and is a great fishing lake. The reason the price is high is because this lot is on the big lake side of the peninsula. The lots on the other side of the road face a smaller bay and are less expensive."

"Let's look at those lots," commented Dave.

We walked back to the car and drove up the hill around the large oak tree in the middle of the road. There were two beautiful lots right next to each other overlooking the smaller bay. One of them was flat, wooded, and good sized, and the other had a slight grade to it. Parking our cars on the road, we made our way through the dense foliage to the lakeshore where a cluster of beautiful Norway pines stood tall and stately. The lots were elevated from the water, and the view was magnificent. The water was still crystal clear, but there were some weeds and vegetation growing near the shore.

"What do you think, Bob?" I questioned as he and I were standing together on the shoreline.

"I love this lot, Tommy! Do you think it's too expensive?"

I called Jon, Don, and Steve over. We all agreed that this would be a perfect place to build a cabin. We were some of the first people to look at these lots.

"What a find!" I stated staring into Jon's eyes. "This bay has to be loaded with huge bass."

"Tommy, I want this property," Jon said with glistening eyes.

"So do I, Jon. So do I."

Dave called us back to the car. He had been talking to Fred.

"Get into the car. We're going back to the office," he said.

As we headed back to Siren, Dave asked, "What do you think of this lot, guys?"

"I love it, Dave," I responded.

My brothers all responded the same way.

"You won't believe what they're asking for it," whispered Dave with a smirk on his face.

"It's too expensive," stated Bob with a frown.

"They want seven hundred dollars! We have one thousand dollars, so I think we should buy two lots. We'll pay cash for one, put three hundred dollars down on the other, and pay off the rest on time payments."

"I can't believe the price," I stated in awe.

"This is perfect for us," confirmed Dave. "First of all, it's on a peninsula with a private road. That means it will be away from traffic. It will be quiet and very private. Secondly, the lake is a good size, has character, and is clean and very deep."

"What do you mean by character?" questioned Steve.

"It isn't just a round boring lake," Dave replied. "North Sand Lake has inlets, bays, marshes, and character."

"I understand, Dave. Character means that it's interesting with a lot of variety," responded Steve.

"Exactly," responded Dave.

We were all excited and could hardly wait to get to the real estate office. When we arrived, Dave bought the two lots. He paid cash for one and put three hundred dollars down on the other.

Our payments would be about thirty-one dollars a month to pay off the second lot in one year. That spring evening in 1963, the Hall boys drove back to Minneapolis as proud owners of not one but two gorgeous lots on a fantastic lake. And, it was just a hundred and ten miles away from our home. Little did we realize what an amazing decision we had just made together. It would become an adventure of a lifetime for us boys, and I believe it was God's gift to our family. I only wish Dad could have been involved with our decision.

OUR FIRST SUMMER

The property we Hall boys had purchased was on an outstanding lake in Burnett County just outside of Webster, Wisconsin. Our first summer up there in 1963, we were not children anymore. Sibling rivalry had run its course. We had been very competitive as children growing up. Now, as young men, we faced together the new challenge of clearing our land and preparing our lot to build a cabin.

Dave was now twenty-nine and working as a teacher and hockey coach at Edison High School. I was twenty-one and engaged to be married in September. Bob was nineteen years old and taking classes at a trade school. Jon was seventeen and a junior in high school. Don was fifteen and about to be a sophomore in high school, and Steve was thirteen and just finishing seventh grade. We had lots of manpower to work our property, but we didn't have much knowledge. My younger brothers and I depended on Dave to be our leader as to how to go about this new project of ours.

We journeyed to our lake lot many times that summer, especially on weekends. When we arrived at our lot on our very first trip, I hopped out of Dave's car and just stared at our newly purchased possession. As I surveyed the landscape, I noticed thick shrubs, multiple trees and saplings, and vegetation of every kind totally covering the land. It was about as dense and thick as any forest could be. I scratched my head while observing the spectacle before us. Then, I made a brilliant statement.

"Well, guys, where do we begin?"

"To start with," Dave suggested, "we need to get the tools out of the trunk."

Dave was an Industrial Arts teacher and had access to a lot of tools. Jon opened the back of Dave's station wagon and began taking out tools. He laid them on the side of the road.

"Don't just stand there, guys. Help Jon with our equipment," Dave ordered.

We all helped unload the car. Dave had brought shovels, rakes, saws, cutting tools, cycles, axes, and various other hand tools used for clearing brush.

"The first thing we need to do is cut a road into our place," instructed Dave. "This little clearing is in the middle of our two lots. We can begin here and make a 'Y' shaped road that goes into both lots."

I stared at the little opening Dave described. It was filled with small shrubs, plants of various kinds, weeds, and thick brush. I grabbed the shovel and dug out a shrub. The soil was sandy, so it came out fairly easily.

"At least the soil is sandy," I shouted. "I'll use the shovel to dig out these smaller plants. Some of you will need to use axes to chop out the thick roots. The rest of you can use rakes to pick up the loose material and the cutting shears to cut branches and vines out of the way."

"This looks like quite a project," announced Bob as he picked up a rake.

All six of us began hacking, chopping, and digging our way through the dense brush.

"We should have brought leather gloves. My hands are beginning to get blisters already!" yelled Jon.

It was a sight to see. We all worked very hard swinging and chopping our way into our lot. We cleared everything in our way. We were all pretty strong and in good shape because we were involved in sports. But, we were not used to this hard labor. After working for about three hours, we had cleared a road about halfway into our newly acquired property.

"Time to take a break, guys," Dave yelled.

We dropped our tools and observed our progress. We saw the beginnings of our road. It was about five feet wide with a sand bottom and thick vegetation on each side.

"It doesn't look too bad," I stated after seeing our progress.

"Tommy, pull my station wagon into our road and get it out of the way," shouted Dave.

"Will do, big brother!" I yelled back as I headed for his vehicle.

"Don, go with Tom and get the basket of food Mom made for us. Bring it over to the clearing by the lake," Dave ordered.

I pulled Dave's station wagon into our lot, and Don brought the basket of food to my hungry brothers. We sat in a circle next to one of the big Norway pines. Don spread out a blanket and put the basket of food on top of it. Bob prayed for the meal, thanking the Lord for the food and for blessing us brothers with this beautiful spot.

"Help yourself, guys!" shouted Dave as he pulled a sandwich from the basket.

Mom had fixed us a great lunch with sandwiches, apples, chips, and a dessert. We also had a thermos of coffee and hot chocolate. We were starved after working so hard. After I was done eating, I leaned my back against the trunk of one of the huge Norway pines and surveyed the scenery. I was sitting about fifteen feet above the water. Below me sat our sandy beach and the clear blue water. The bay was much smaller than the main lake and contained a lot of weeds and bull rushes. There were many lily pads just beginning to bloom. Across the bay was an opening which appeared to be a large marsh of some kind. There were no buildings or cabins across the bay.

"What direction is it across the water?" I asked.

"West, Tommy," responded Dave as he was getting up from his spot on the ground. "That means we'll be able to observe beautiful sunsets from this vantage point."

"I love it up here, Tommy," said Jon. "When can we go fishing?"

"There will be plenty of time for that, Jon," stated Dave overhearing Jon's question and raising his voice so we all could hear. "Today, we have plenty of work to do. We will all work and all play together. If there is work to do, then we'll all pitch in. When the work is done, then we can all fish, play, relax, or do whatever we want. That is kind of how it will work up here."

"Do you think we can build as nice a cabin as Keith's parents did?" asked Steve.

"I've got something in mind because I've been doing some research on lake cabins. I think whatever we build should fit right into the land and not look too traditional. But, before we build our cabin, I think we should build a boathouse."

"Why should we build a boathouse first, Dave?" asked Jon. "We don't even have a boat."

"I have a friend who has some property on Lake Minnetonka. He built a boathouse and has been using it until he can afford to build a cabin. I think we should do the same."

"Do you know how to build a boathouse, Dave?" asked Don.

"I have an idea," Dave replied. "We would first dig out the side of the hill facing the lake. We would then order some cement blocks and have some cement delivered for the floor of the boathouse. We would pour the floor, trowel it out so it was smooth, and build up the walls with the blocks. It would have a flat roof and would be a place to sleep in until we could afford to build a cabin."

"It sounds like a plan," Bob said.

"Now, we need to get back to work because that road won't get done by itself," I stated trying to sound like my big brother.

"Good job, Tommy!" yelled Dave as we all headed back to our project.

We worked very hard for the rest of the day and completed our sandy road. As we finished the project, the sun began to set over the far side of the bay. There was a bright red color in the sky, and the sun appeared very large in the horizon. The sight was magnificent, and the moment was significant for us. We loaded up Dave's station wagon and drove home.

Most of our trips that summer were spent working or clearing the land. It was hard work. After building our driveway, Dave bought all of us leather work gloves to protect our hands. We cleared out a nice area where we could set up tents and build a campfire. We could then stay overnight.

One weekend, instead of clearing the land, Dave had us sink a well and build an outhouse. I was on well duty with Dave and Steve. Dave had ordered some three inch pipe with connectors and a sand point. We fastened the sand point to the pipe, put a wooden block on top of the pipe so we wouldn't ruin the threads, and began pounding it into the ground with a sledgehammer. I pounded while Steve held the wood block on the pipe. As a section reached the surface of the ground, we threaded on another section and continued hammering.

"You better not miss, Tommy," remarked Steve as I swung the sledgehammer.

"Just hold that block of wood on the end, and I'll pound on the opposite side. I'll be careful, little brother," I assured him.

After we were down about thirty feet, Dave suggested that we stop.

"We may be in a vane of water, so let's give it a try."

"How are we going to do that?" questioned Steve.

"We'll just screw this hand pump on tight and see if we get any water," responded Dave.

Dave put some gray material on the pipe and began screwing on the red pump by hand until it was secure.

"What's that stuff you put on the pipe?" I asked.

"Pipe dope."

"What does that do?" questioned Steve.

"It seals up the connection so we won't have any leaks," answered Dave.

"You're sure smart, Dave," added Steve.

"I've never been accused of that," he responded as he looked at me and winked. "Start pumping, Tom."

I grabbed the short handle of the pump and began pumping. Dave poured water down the pipe after each stroke to prime the pump. As I was pumping, we heard a gurgling sound. All of a sudden, water came gushing out of the spout.

"I guess we have water, Tom!" yelled Steve with a gleam in his eye.

"Is it drinkable?" I asked.

"Bring me a cup from the car, Steve," ordered Dave.

When Steve returned with the cup, I pumped as Dave held the cup in front of the spout. Water gushed out and filled the cup to overflowing. Dave took a little sip and then swallowed the water with one big gulp.

"Do you want to taste our water, Tom?" asked Dave. "It's cold and delicious!"

I pumped some more, and Steve and I agreed that the water tasted very good and refreshing. Dave went to his car and brought back a jar with a cover on it.

"Pump some water, Tommy."

Dave filled up the jar and put the lid on it.

"What are you doing?" I questioned.

"I am going to bring this sample back to the University of Minnesota. We'll have it tested just to make sure it is pure, but I already believe it is."

"Boy, Dave! You think of everything," shouted Steve.

"You can never be too safe, little brother," responded Dave.

While Dave, Steve, and I were finding water and drilling our well, Bob, Jon, and Don were putting up an outhouse on the south side of our lot close to the property line. They dug a fairly deep hole and built a box over it. They cut a round hole on top of the box and secured a toilet seat over it. Then, they built a small building around the box, hung a door, and put on a roof that only angled to one side. After that, they placed tar paper on the roof and sealed it with some kind of caulk. Now, we were proud owners of an outhouse and had water from our hand pump.

Before leaving to go home each trip, we would always stand back to examine our work and all we had done. We were amazed at what we had done by ourselves and so in awe that this really was "our" lake property.

BUILDING THE BOATHOUSE

When we returned to our lake lot the next summer in 1964, it felt very fulfilling to turn onto the driveway we had completed and see all we had accomplished on our lot. We again unloaded Dave's station wagon and placed all the tools for our next project on the ground. Then, we began putting up two tents in the clearing we had made for them. We planned to spend the weekend digging out the side of the hill for our boathouse. When the tents were done, we each grabbed some tools and headed down by the water to survey our target.

"It doesn't look like an easy project, Dave," I stated as I scanned the hill.

The spot we were eyeing was a hill about fifteen feet high and full of vegetation. There were bushes, small trees, and plants of all kinds.

"It's called manpower, Tommy. We'll need to clear all the vegetation before we can begin to dig," responded Dave.

"How are we going to do that?" questioned Jon as he scratched his head and observed the mammoth project ahead of us.

"We will attack this hill by chopping, cutting, digging, and clearing," stated Dave as he picked up the ax and began chopping down a small tree.

And that's what we did, attack the hill. It was a sight for sore eyes. We each grabbed a particular tool and spread out like little ants. We removed all the vegetation that covered the hill. We each wore the leather gloves Dave had purchased for us. We had learned our lesson after coming home with blistered hands when we cleared the brush for our road. Some of us dug out plants with shovels while others sawed branches and cut small vines. We all chopped and dug out the roots which seemed to be everywhere. It took us all day to clear an area just a little bigger than the size of a single car garage. After finishing our work, we gathered at the bottom of the hill to admire our accomplishment.

"It's amazing. There is nothing left on that hill except sand," stated Bob.

"It's not so amazing when every bone in my body is hurting," complained Jon.

"You guys worked hard, so we can rest for the night. Tomorrow may be even worse as we dig into that hill to make room for our boathouse," Dave stated as he walked up the hill heading for the station wagon.

"Grab all the tools, guys. We need to put them in Dave's car in case it rains tonight," I shouted.

We gathered all our tools and placed them in the station wagon.

"Tom, I want you to start a fire because Marilyn sent up some hamburgers to roast on the grill. Bob, you help Tom with the fire. The rest of you guys help me get ready for dinner," ordered Dave.

"Where do we start, Tom?" asked Bob.

"We need some birch bark, some small twigs, and some kindling to start the fire. I'll saw some of the larger wood into sections and split them. Then, we can get a good hot cooking fire."

Bob began gathering the kindling, and I found a log about four inches in diameter that we had chopped from the hill. First, I stripped off all the little branches. It was about six feet long, so I sawed it into two foot sections and split them in halves. Bob found some rocks on the beach and made a circle for the firepit in a small clearing. He also collected a stack of kindling. When I finished chopping the wood, I carried the logs and piled them by our firepit. We placed the birch bark in the center of the rocks, piled the small branches and twigs on top, and surrounded the kindling with the split logs in a teepee style.

"Where did you learn to set up a fire like that?" questioned Bob.

"I learned it in Boy Scouts," I responded.

"When were you in Boy Scouts, Tom?"

"I joined a troop with my friend, Bruce, at Our Redeemer Lutheran Church. I didn't stay in too long, but we went on a couple of overnights and had to make campfires."

Soon, we had a blazing fire that burned down to glistening embers. The sun was beginning to set, and twilight was descending upon us. After the fire burned down, Dave set up a portable grill. Jon and Don set up the food on a card table along with the paper plates and napkins. Dave tended to the hamburgers sizzling over the hot coals. We also had a kettle of beans cooking on the fire. Mom had sent some potato salad in a cooler, and we had plenty of soda pop. As we sat around the fire, we could hardly wait for the meal to be ready. We were famished!

"Get a bun and come over to the fire. I'll give you a burger," Dave yelled.

We all grabbed a bun and put it on a paper plate. Dave took a cooked burger off the grill with a spatula and placed it on the half bun we held out before him. We put mustard and ketchup on our burgers, spooned the beans and potato salad onto our plates, opened a bottle of pop, and found a place to sit and satisfy our hunger. None of us said much as we wolfed down the food. It was a delicious dinner, and we ate our fill. After supper, we cleaned up, washed the pot in the lake, and put all the garbage in a bag and placed it in Dave's car. We all strolled back to the campfire, found a place to sit, watched the fire, and just relaxed. Full and satisfied, I gazed into the sky and watched the stars begin to appear as the sky darkened. I loved being in this place with my brothers. Steve came over and sat by me.

"How are you doing, little brother?" I asked.

"That was a great dinner, Tommy. I was starved."

"I was too, but I feel better now."

"I love it up here. It's so quiet and peaceful. Will you sleep with me tonight?" asked Steve.

"Sure! I'll put my sleeping bag right next to yours."

As the night began to slip over us, I gazed at the setting around us. We were in deep, thick woods overlooking a small bay with the sun setting on the far horizon. The stars began to multiply as the sky grew darker and the fire burned low. We all listened to the sounds of nature in an environment that was totally strange to each of us. We were on a journey and had no idea where it would take us.

"Can you believe this is our very own property!" stated Don.

"Yeah! No one can kick us off our own land," added Jon.

"This is for Dad," proclaimed Dave. "Even though he can't be here, it's for him. He always wanted to retire at a lake home. Now, we are going to make that dream come true. Even though we can't see him, somehow I believe he can see us and is smiling."

Tears began flowing down my cheeks.

"What's the matter, Tommy?" questioned Steve.

"I miss Dad! I wasn't a very good son. I just want to tell him how sorry I am."

"We all miss him, Tommy," responded Dave. "I guess I knew him the best because I'm the oldest. It was hard for me to get married just one month after he died. I was going to call off the wedding but changed my mind when I realized he wouldn't want me to do that."

"I think we all miss Dad," stated Bob. "It has been a hard time for our family, especially Mom."

"She was really acting strange for a long time," added Jon. "Thankfully, she's doing much better now."

"You know, growing up in a large family, we were all competitive and had our differences. But today, as we were all working together clearing that hill, I realized how lucky we are to be brothers," I said.

"Yeah!" stated Jon. "We weren't fighting or arguing. We were just working our butts off to clear that hill!"

"I'm afraid we're not done yet," Dave said. "Tomorrow, we have an even bigger project ahead of us as we dig out that hill by hand. And, I have some bad news. My back is really bothering me. I'm afraid that I won't be of much help."

"What's the matter with your back?" asked Don.

"I don't know if I pulled a muscle or what. After we were done working, I could hardly straighten up. Maybe it will be better in the morning. Tommy, I want you to put out the fire. We all need to get a good night's rest so we can finish that hill tomorrow. I've already ordered the blocks and the cement truck for next weekend."

"We'll get it done, Dave. There are still five healthy, strong Hall boys left to complete this project." I responded.

As the others went to their tents to cash in for the night, I grabbed the kettle and headed for the lake to fill it with water. When I came back up the hill, everyone was in bed. I spread out the burning coals with a stick and poured water on our campfire. It hissed and steamed as the fire refused to go out. I went back to the lake for more water. After three attempts, I finally won the battle. I placed my bare hand in the wet wood to make sure the fire was truly out. It was. I crawled into my tent and found Steve already asleep. I rolled up in my sleeping bag.

"Good night, Tom," Bob whispered.

"Yeah, good night, Bob," I replied.

When I awoke the next morning, Steve and Bob were still sound asleep. I rolled out of my sleeping bag, dressed, and crawled out of the tent. Dave was up and standing in front of the firepit.

"Good morning, Tommy. Could you get a fire going, and I'll get the breakfast ready?"

"Sure, Dave. What are we having for breakfast?"

"French toast, bacon, coffee, and hot chocolate."

"Sounds good. I'll cut up some more wood and get a good fire going."

Soon the fire was blazing. As it burned down, Dave put the portable grill over the fire. He soaped up the bottom of the frying pan and placed it on the grill.

"What are you doing, Dave?" I questioned.

"We have to clean this pan after we're done eating. If you soap the bottom, it makes it much easier to clean. You just use some SOS pads, and it cleans right up nice and easy."

"Hey, that's a great idea. I'm glad I thought of it."

"Good, because it will be your job to clean up after we're all done eating," Dave said with a smirk on his face.

After our fill of French toast smothered with syrup, bacon, and toast with peanut butter, I poured myself a cup of steaming hot coffee. I sat next to a pine tree and drank in the scenery. It was a cool morning with a slight breeze. Everyone was sitting around either drinking coffee or hot chocolate. Dave and Bob were drinking coffee and involved in a deep conversation. Jon, Don, and Steve were all together and laughing uncontrollably while I was gazing out on the lake deep in my own thoughts.

"I really can't believe this is happening," I thought as I drank my last sip of coffee. "I feel like I'm on a camping trip, only this isn't a camping trip. This is our very own property. What did we ever do to deserve this?"

"Thank you, God, for this beautiful place," I prayed out loud very softly. "May it become a place to hold our family together. It frightens me to think I almost blew it by buying those golf clubs. I am grateful that Dave gave me another chance. Please help us, Father, as we grow, get married, and have children to come here and remain a close family as we grow old together. I feel like the most blessed man in the world."

"Tommy, take the pan and coffee pot down to the lake and clean them," Dave called interrupting my silence. "There are some SOS pads in a bag on the front seat of my car."

"Will do," I shouted back.

"The rest of you guys grab the shovels from my car. Let's get after that hill," ordered Dave.

Everyone cleaned up their area and put their trash in a bag. I grabbed the SOS pads and headed down to the lake. I sat on a rock and dipped the pan into the water. I couldn't believe how quickly the cooking pan cleaned up with that soap on the bottom. I cleaned the frying pan and coffee pot so well they were both shining when I was finished.

"How's this, Dave?" I asked showing him the fruits of my labor.

"Fine, Tom. Now, get a shovel and help your brothers. I'm afraid all I can do is supervise today. My back is killing me."

I grabbed a shovel. My brothers were really tearing into the hill. With most of the vegetation gone, the work wasn't too bad because the sand was soft. Once in a while, we had to chop out roots and vines. We all worked very hard and managed to dig out the hill in about ten hours. We loaded a lot of the sand into a wheelbarrow and threw it on the shoreline. The rest of the sand we just threw to the side.

After we finished, we stood back to examine our work. We had dug back into the hill about fifteen to twenty feet. It was all cleared out and ready for our boathouse to be created. As we were standing and admiring our work, Jon walked into the cavity that we had created.

"Wow, I can't believe we did all this work."

Just as he finished that sentence, the top of the hill came crumbling down and almost buried Jon. We all stood in amazement. Jon was up to his shoulders in sand. He was pinned in and couldn't move.

"Hey, guys, a little help would be appreciated!" he yelled.

We just stared in amazement. Finally, I grabbed a shovel and began to move toward him. Don grabbed my arm.

"Leave him there, Tom," he said.

"What do you mean, Don? We have to dig him out."

"He'll be all right," stated Dave. "Let's go have some supper."

"Yeah, let him suffer for a while," threw in Steve. "It will serve him right for the way he's bugged us all our lives."

"All right, guys," I said as I dropped my shovel.

We all turned and began walking up the hill to eat our supper.

"Hey, this isn't funny!" screamed Jon.

"You'll be fine, little brother. We'll dig you out after supper," I stated.

We went up to our little cleared area and began eating our supper, all the while listening to

Jon threaten us. He finally realized he was at our mercy until after supper and shut up. Dave kept a close watch on the hill to make sure there weren't any more cave-ins. After supper, we strolled back down to our project. Jon just stared at us in disbelief.

"Now, you know how we feel after you keep us awake all night and treat us like slaves, Jon," Don shouted.

"I'm going to get you for this!" yelled Jon as he glared at Steve and Don.

"Let's leave him there for a little while longer!" shouted Steve with a smirk on his face.

It was interesting to see Jon so helpless. He was so used to being in control and calling the shots.

"All right, guys, dig your brother out," Dave said.

We all got shovels and had Jon uncovered in about ten minutes. He had cooled down now that he was free.

"That wasn't funny, guys. I owe you big time!"

"Promises, promises," I stated as I wiped the sand off of his clothes. "You've got to see the humor in this, Jon. You guys would have done the same to me."

"I guess it was kind of funny," responded Jon as his eyes softened.

"Just think of the wonderful memory you created for us. Maybe someday, I'll write it in a book," I commented with a sly look on my face.

"Yeah, right! That will be some day when you write a book, Tommy," Jon smarted back.

"There are some sandwiches and pop left for you on the table," stated Dave.

Jon strolled to the top of the hill to eat his supper while we cleared out the rest of the sand. Everything was ready to start building our boathouse the next weekend.

We drove back to our lake lot the next weekend. After unloading the car, we walked down to the lakeshore to examine our project. The hill was as we had left it and ready for the cement truck. While we waited for the cement truck to arrive, Dave gathered us in a circle.

"How's your back, Dave?" I questioned.

"It's much better. I think I will be able to pitch in this weekend."

"What's the plan?" asked Bob.

"When the truck arrives, he will back in on our neighbor's road. I've already gotten Harold's permission to use his road. The truck will back to the top of the hill and drop a chute down to the site of our boathouse. I will direct him where to pour. Tom and Jon will have rubber boots on. They will push the wet cement around so it fills to the top of the two by fours I put in last week. They will push the cement and make it as even as they can to the top of the forms. Bob and Don will take this long two-by-four and go back and forth over the cement until it is uniform. After that, I will get some small pieces of plywood and start from the back and work forward with a trowel to make it smooth."

"Have you ever done this before, Dave?" I questioned.

"No, but a friend of mine is a block layer, and he told me what to do."

"I hope it all turns out," stated Bob with a worried look on his face.

Just then, the cement truck pulled to the front of our lot. The big drum was turning round and round mixing the fresh cement. Dave talked to the driver and had him back his truck up to the top of the hill and drop his chute. Jon and I moved to the base ready to do our part. We had on our rubber boots and were ready when the cement came pouring down. We directed the cement to various parts of the base by moving the chute. When the cement filled the base, we pushed it around to make it as even as possible. It took a lot of strength and stamina to move the heavy wet cement. Don and Bob took a large two-by-four and pulled the cement so it was level with the top of the forms. Then, they moved the two-by-four back and forth to smooth out the cement. Finally, Dave moved to the back of the slab and began troweling the cement to make it very smooth. He worked his way to the front and did an outstanding job. We finished off the project by making a three foot apron in front with a slight angle to the lake. After the job was completed, we were not only amazed but impressed with our project.

"I can't believe you never did cement work before, Dave. You looked like you knew exactly what you were doing," I said slapping him on the back.

"It's not quite professional, but it doesn't look too bad," responded Dave as he examined his work. "Once I got the hang of using the trowel, it seemed to go better."

"I hope it doesn't rain so it can dry smoothly," stated Bob.

We all stood on the beach and admired our work. We were impressed with our effort because we had never constructed anything before. It was a team effort. It was very satisfying to begin our first project on our newly acquired property. We gathered all the tools, loaded up the station wagon, cleaned up all the debris, and headed for home.

"I'm having the blocks delivered from Hopkins Cement Company this coming week," explained Dave as we drove home.

"Do you know how to lay blocks, Dave?" questioned Don.

"I have a good idea, and I'll explain your roles when we come back next weekend."

We were all pretty quiet as we drove home exhausted from all the work we had done. It was fun, exciting, and satisfying to work together on a project that we all owned.

The next weekend, we arrived at our lake lot to find the cement slab had dried nicely. The cement blocks had been delivered and stacked in neat piles toward the front of our lot. Dave delegated our duties as we began building the walls of our boathouse with the blocks. Jon and Steve were in charge of bringing the blocks down to the beach. They would load them into the wheelbarrow and stack them at the front of the boathouse. Bob and Don were in charge of mixing the cement that we placed between the blocks to make them secure. Dave and I were laying the blocks.

"Tom, in order to get the cement blocks straight, we need to snap a chalk line to line up the first row," Dave stated.

Dave measured equal distances in from the sides of the slab and made several marks with a piece of yellow chalk. Next, he had me pull a chalk line from a container that held the line. When I pulled out the string, I noticed it was covered with blue chalk. We each held an end as I walked to one side of the cement slab, and Dave walked to the other side.

"Hold your end on the mark, Tommy. You need to hold it tight."

He put his end on a mark and stretched the string until it was tight. Then, he raised the string and let it snap back down. A blue imprint was left on the cement which made a perfectly straight line. Dave and I made lines all the way around the rectangle.

Don and Bob came down with a load of cement they had mixed in another wheelbarrow Dave had borrowed from a neighbor. Dave demonstrated how to lay the cement blocks. He put some cement down with a trowel and smoothed it out. Next, he placed a block down and then placed a level on top of it. When the bubble was directly in the middle, the block was level.

"I'll work on this side, and you work on the opposite side," Dave ordered. "You must make sure the blocks are straight and level, Tom."

Steve and Jon supplied the blocks, and Don and Bob kept the cement coming. Slowly, the work progressed. As I began laying the blocks, I realized it wasn't as easy as it looked. Dave was almost finished with his row, while I just had a few blocks laid.

"Dave, how do you lay the blocks so fast? I'm really struggling to keep them level."

"Don't try to keep up with me. Just keep doing the best that you can, Tom. It will get easier as you continue."

However, the truth was, it wasn't getting easier. It was getting harder. I just didn't seem to have the knack for laying blocks and keeping them level. When Don brought me the next load of cement, he realized I was struggling.

"Let me try laying the blocks, Tom," he offered.

"Be my guest," I responded.

Don took to it right away. He would trowel cement onto the slab, place the block on top, and level it by tapping one end and removing the cement in certain places until it was level.

"This isn't so difficult, Tom," stated Don. "You help Bob mix cement, and I'll lay the blocks."

"Is that all right, Dave?" I questioned.

"If Don's better at it than you, let him have at it."

So, Don and I switched roles. When I walked down a few minutes later with another load of wet cement, I watched Don in amazement. He was catching up to Dave. The sides and the back of the boathouse were taking shape.

Don looked like a professional block layer as he laid block after block. With minor adjustments, he would make the blocks straight and level. We worked until about one o'clock, and the sides and back on the boathouse were about three quarters finished. Dave and Don were doing a great job laying the blocks, and the rest of us provided the grunt labor.

"Let's take a break, guys, and have some lunch," Dave stated.

We used up the last of the mixed cement and laid a few more blocks. After washing up in the lake, we headed to our little clearing for lunch.

"I can't believe how well our project is going," stated Dave.

"Do you think we'll finish today?" asked Bob.

"I think we'll finish the block work today, but the front and roof will be a little trickier," responded Dave.

"It's important that we keep the blocks staggered because that's what gives the walls strength," stated Don.

"Where did you learn to lay blocks like that, Donny?" questioned Steve.

"Just by doing it and watching Dave," explained Don.

"As hard as I tried, I couldn't seem to get the hang of it. Thanks for coming to my rescue," I replied.

"No problem, Tom. We each have different gifts. I just happen to find this easy, so thanks for letting me take your place."

"You're welcome, Don. It is a lot easier for me to keep the cement mixed and ready when you need it," I replied.

That afternoon, we completed laying all the blocks in rows of twelve. On the top row, Dave had us place long bolts into the wet cement. When the cement dried, the bolts would stick up. That would enable us to later secure wooden beams in place by drilling holes and bolting them to the blocks. It was a very hot day, and we were covered with sweat and very dirty.

"Let's go for a swim," I suggested.

At the very mention of jumping into the cool clear water of North Sand Lake, my brothers ran for their swimming suits. We changed into our suits on our lot without any thought of modesty. We grabbed our towels, hung them around our necks, and headed for the point. The point was a beautiful lot at the end of the peninsula that hadn't sold yet. It was the most expensive lot on the lake, selling for seven thousand dollars. We loved to swim at the point because there was a big drop off. About fifteen feet out in the lake, the bottom sharply dropped down to forty feet. We loved that because we were all excellent swimmers.

When we reached the point, we dropped our towels and dove into the clear blue, spring fed water. It was a spectacular sight underwater. The water was so clear and pure that we could keep our eyes open. I was the last one in. As I dove underwater, I clearly observed my brothers diving deep into the drop off area. They had bubbles all around them. After a deep dive, Jon surfaced and let out a yell of delight that spoke for all of us. We were in sheer ecstasy after a grueling day of hard labor. We kept surfacing for air and diving deeper each time. The water was so clear that when I held my hand in front of my face, it was as visible as if it was out of the water. I only wish I had an underwater camera to capture all the joy we had. After about an hour, we finally got tired and headed back to our lot and nearly built boathouse.

That night after supper, we just relaxed and went to bed early. The next day, we checked the blocks. They had dried nicely and looked very straight and level. We were very proud of our work. We all felt pretty exhausted as we packed up and headed back home.

We drove back to our lot again the next weekend. We built a flat roof on our boathouse and installed a garage door. Next to the garage door, we hung an entrance door with a window in it. When all the jobs were completed, we had erected a pretty nice boathouse. As we gathered the tools, I admired our project.

"I can't believe we did all this work by ourselves in just a few weekends, Dave," I stated in amazement.

"We'll have to roof it next," responded Dave.

"How are we going to do that?" questioned Jon.

"I'll get rolls of roofing paper. We'll roll them out and caulk the seams. It shouldn't be too difficult."

"I'm sure glad we have you, Dave. We would be in big trouble without you," Bob acknowledged.

"I couldn't do all this work alone. We need each other to make all this happen for us," Dave also acknowledged. "Before we leave, we'll need to fill in the spaces behind the blocks with all that sand we piled on the hill."

We all grabbed our shovels and dumped the sand back behind the blocks until it was all tight and nicely packed. I couldn't believe how great our boathouse turned out. Now, we didn't need to bring up tents anymore. We could just sleep in our boathouse when we came to work.

After our boathouse was finished, we were very busy clearing more of our land. We tried to leave as many trees as possible but did take down some birch, maple and cherry trees. Dave discovered a lumbermill not far from our lot that would pick up our logs, saw them into lumber, and dry and cure them for us. We planned to use them for the walls inside our cabin. That was Dave's idea. We also discussed where to build the cabin.

Toward the end of summer, Dave called the electric company and had them bring in electric power to our property. They placed the electric meter on a post. Dave and Bob then wired our boathouse, so we had electricity there. Now, we could light the boathouse and put in a small refrigerator as well.

By the end of the summer, our densely wooded lot began to take shape. We had cleared an area for our future cabin site. After we cleared the area, we had thrown down grass seed. By the end of August, we actually had a pretty nice lawn established. We left the back part of the lot wild because it provided a little buffer from the road and gave us some privacy. All in all, it was a good summer for the Hall brothers. We learned to work hard and love one another. It was a summer I will never forget!

One day as we were all enjoying the lake, Dave got us brothers together with another idea. As we sat together on top of the flat roof of the boathouse on lawn chairs, Dave explained his idea.

"Guys, I think we should sell the lot next to us."

"Dave, that is the nicest of the two lots. It is flat and filled with beautiful trees. We can't sell that lot," replied Bob.

"I agree with Bob. That is a choice lot, and we shouldn't sell it," I added.

The others shook their heads in agreement with us.

"We can't sell this lot because we've built this nice boathouse already," responded Dave.

"Why do we have to sell the lot?" question Steve.

"So we can buy the lot across the road on the big lake side," answered Dave.

We all just stared at each other in amazement. We sat there kind of stunned by what Dave had just suggested. Finally, Bob broke the ice.

"Can we afford the lot on the other side of the peninsula, Dave?"

"I've already looked into it. I have someone who will give us eight hundred dollars for this lot, and we can purchase that lot for two thousand five hundred dollars," responded Dave.

"If we put the eight hundred dollars down on that lot, we will still owe one thousand seven hundred dollars," offered Bob.

"That's right, little brother, and we can pay off that loan in a few years."

"But, that lot doesn't have many trees," complained Jon.

"There are trees on the front and back of the lot, but you're right, Jon. The lot is pretty much bare and sandy," answered Dave.

"We can plant trees," I responded as I was being persuaded to Dave's point of view. "Have you seen the beach on that lot? It's gorgeous and sandy!"

"Yeah, with no weeds," added Don.

"We would have this lot to fish and that lot to swim and water ski," added Jon as he came to see the potential of Dave's suggestion.

"Let's go for it, Dave. I'm surprised no one has purchased that lot yet. We better grab it before someone else does," I suggested.

"I don't know, Tom. Two thousand five hundred dollars is a lot of money," responded Bob.

"It isn't two thousand five hundred dollars, Bob," I exclaimed. "It is actually one thousand seven hundred dollars when we sell this lot. I think it's a great deal. I say let's go for it!"

"What do you all think?" questioned Dave.

Suddenly, we all were unified and gave Dave the green light to sell our lot next door and purchase the lot on the big lake side. This did happen in the spring of 1965. Dave sold our empty lot for eight hundred dollars to an older gentleman named Joe Roban and purchased the lot on the big side of the lake through Lakes Real Estate in Siren for two thousand five hundred dollars. Our payments were about fifty-four dollars a month for three years to pay off the one thousand seven hundred dollars owed after putting down eight hundred dollars. This decision to buy on the big lake would prove to be one of the best ones we would ever make.

LIFE AT THE BOATHOUSE

By the summer of 1965, we Hall boys had two lots, one on the back bay and one on the big lake. One was paid for, and we were paying off the big lake lot. Our one room boathouse, with its cement floor and block walls, was completed on the bay lot and all paid off. When we came up to the lake, we had a place to sleep, water to drink from our outside hand pump, and an outhouse. It wasn't much, but we felt like the wealthiest men on earth.

We spent many wonderful weekends at the lake even though we didn't have a cabin built yet. We would pack some food, drive the two hours from Minneapolis, and spend the weekend working on our lots, swimming, fishing, and eventually water skiing. We often sat on the flat roof of our boathouse just enjoying the view over the back bay and the smells and sounds of the Wisconsin woods. We were all as happy as a lark because we had a roof over our heads to keep us dry and warm, and it was our own lake place.

Our one room boathouse was about the size of an extended single garage. It had electricity but no running water. We had to walk outside up the hill to the hand pump to get water. If we needed hot water, we had to boil it. We did not have a stove, but probably had an electric hot plate. Otherwise, we cooked outside on our charcoal grill. We also had to walk up the hill to the outhouse to go potty. We had lights and would plug in a big fan in the hot summer. There were no windows. We would pull up the garage door during the day for fresh air and light. It had to be closed at night because of mosquitos.

Against the back wall in the boathouse we had a compact unit that had a small refrigerator in it. The top had a small sink on one side that we couldn't use and a drain board on the other. Underneath was the refrigerator on one half and storage on the other. We still have this unit in our garage today for storing worms and fish bait. The boathouse was the only place to store things. Stuff like fish poles and tackle, life jackets, water skis, lawn chairs, tools, our suitcases, and food we brought was lying all around.

There was no furniture in the boathouse. We did have an old folding card table and chairs we used for eating or playing games. Folding lawn chairs were all we had for sitting. We used cots and lawn chairs that folded out flat for sleeping. It was pretty comfortable snuggling in our sleeping bags on top of them. We did have one bigger rollaway bed which our mother used when she came up. One night, Janet, Jon's girl-friend now wife, volunteered to sleep in the bed with Mom. Mom snored so loud that Janet could hardly stand it. Somehow, she made it through the night with Mom sawing logs in her face. Jon got an earful the next morning!

We boys were used to tight and not so nice quarters back at home. Crowding into the boathouse was not a big deal for us. We thought everything was great. However, our wives probably have different stories to tell about this endeavor! It wasn't just a few times staying in the boathouse, but every time we went to the lake for five or six years. Despite the circumstances, we always found something to laugh about and made many memories together.

Dave was a high school hockey coach. After we built the boathouse, he saved all the broken hockey sticks during the hockey season. This amounted to quite a few sticks. One weekend, Dave brought them all up to the lake and dumped them in a huge pile.

"What's with all the sticks?" asked Jon.

"What do you think they're for?" responded Dave.

"Maybe they're for building a fence around our property," suggested Steve.

"Nope."

"We could lay them end to end and make a drive-way," threw in Bob.

"Wrong again. These sticks are made of hickory and are very strong. We're going to make a dock out of these hockey sticks."

"You're kidding, right?" stated Jon.

"No, I'm absolutely serious. These sticks will last forever and make a great dock. We'll be the only ones on North Sand Lake with a hockey stick dock."

Thus, our next big project began. We bought two-by-fours at the lumberyard in Webster. The lumberyard cut them into eight foot lengths for us. Then, we cut all the hockey sticks into four foot lengths. We laid all of our two-by-fours on the ground and pieced together five sections of dock. Our finished dock would extend about forty feet into the lake.

"I'm pretty impressed," Bob stated. "I never thought this would work, but it turned out to be a great idea, Dave."

"Let's start nailing the hockey sticks to the sections," Dave replied.

When we tried to pound nails into the hockey sticks, the nails began to bend in the hard wood. Dave figured out that we needed to drill holes through the hockey sticks before we attached them to the two-by-fours. After all of the hockey sticks were nailed on, we attached four tall steel poles and big round bases to each section. We left a small space between each stick so water would run off our dock.

Our new dock was a great addition to our lake place. It soon became our fishing spot. We would catch sunfish and bass mostly, but we also pulled in an occasional walleye, northern, or bullhead. This spot was Jon's dream come true. He was the purest fisherman in our family and knew how to catch them. We enjoyed fresh fish many nights for dinner.

Dave found a used ski boat for us. It was an aluminum Lund boat with a 35 horse Mercury. We bought it in the cities and drove it up to our lake. The ski boat opened up a whole new world for us Hall boys. We could fish with it and water ski. We all learned how to ski and spent hours skiing on the big part of the lake. It was pretty hard getting up behind a 35 horse motor, but we quickly learned how to compensate for that. We all loved to ski!

On one occasion, I was pulling Jon over in the big part of the lake. He was skiing up a storm and having a blast cutting in and out of the wake and doing all kinds of tricks.

"Take me back through the channel!" he yelled. "I want to ski all the way back."

"Okay!" I yelled. "Hang on!"

I raced down the lake and into our small back bay. I headed straight for our property and noticed the garage door of our boathouse was wide open. As we approached our shoreline, Jon cut across the wake and headed straight for our lot. He was going way too fast and abruptly hit the shoreline. His feet flew out of his skis, and he went flying into the boathouse. We all gasped.

"He's gonna hit the back wall and get seriously injured!" I screamed.

I turned the boat around and made a beeline for our dock expecting to see Jon splattered against the back wall. As we approached the boathouse, he came strolling out whistling. He had a slight cut on his forehead but was smiling.

"Jon, are you all right?" yelled Steve.

"Yeah. The back wall was a little hard, but I softened the blow," he responded.

Jon always seemed to come out on top regardless of the circumstances or danger. He was, and still is, totally fearless. None of us will forget that incident.

This new experience of owning our own lake place was a dream come true for us Hall boys. We learned to work and play hard together each summer and became close through our journey as co-owners of a common enterprise. We all had something to contribute and different skills to bring to the table. Through it all, we laughed a lot and enjoyed life to the fullest in the incredible setting of North Sand Lake, Wisconsin. I think we're all glad to be a part of this big family and wouldn't want it any other way. All of us learned to love and appreciate one another as we lived out our father's dream.

Another incident happened toward the end of summer in 1965 that would turn out to be very significant. Dave's young son, Danny, was playing in the front of our lot above the boathouse. When we had completed the boathouse, we had filled in the sides and back with sand. However, the sand in the back had settled and left an impression. As Danny was playing near the boathouse, he tripped and fell into the impression. He cut his head, and Dave and Marilyn had trouble stopping the bleeding. For some reason the blood had trouble clotting. They took him to the doctor when they got home and were able to stop the bleeding.

The next spring, Dave stopped by my apartment one afternoon. One look at his face told me something terrible had happened.

"Hi, Dave. Come on in," I suggested as he walked into our apartment with a forlorn expression on his face.

I was married now and living in an apartment with my wife, Sandy. She wasn't home from work yet, so we were all alone.

"Do you want a pop or something?" I asked.

"No."

"What's the matter, Dave? You look like you've just lost your best friend."

"I wish that was the problem, Tom."

My heart began pounding as I gazed into his hurting eyes.

"Marilyn and I brought Danny to the doctor because he wasn't feeling well. We thought it was just the flu or something. They examined him and ran some tests. We received the results of those tests today."

My brother was struggling with his words, and his face was twisted with pain.

"Tommy, my little boy has leukemia."

My heart sank. I didn't even know how to respond. Tears were running down my brother's face. I had never seen him cry before.

"Are they sure?" I questioned.

"Yes, they are absolutely sure!"

"Dave. I'm so sorry," I whispered. "Not Danny, your firstborn! I know how much you love him. He's such a great kid. It's not fair, Dave! It's just not fair! What are you going to do?"

"I'm going to get a second opinion and check out my options."

"I'll pray every night. We need a miracle!"

"Thanks, Tom. I'm open for a miracle. In fact, I'm open for anything."

"How's Marilyn doing?" I questioned.

"She's all broke up, Tom. Pray for her too."

"Absolutely, Dave. If you need anything, just name it. I want to be here for you. Don't hesitate to call any time, day or night."

"Thanks, Tom. We're really hurting and need all the support we can receive right now."

"Have you talked to anyone else in the family?"

"No. You're the first one I've told."

"I'll tell Mom. She will get a prayer chain going, and then I'll tell the brothers and Gwen."

"Thanks, Tom. I'm sorry to be the bearer of bad news."

"Dave, you don't need to walk through this valley alone. Let us do all we can for you and Marilyn."

"Thanks, Tom," whispered Dave as he got up to leave.

As he walked down the stairs and out the door, I stood at the top of the stairs stunned at my brother's news. Dave loved Danny more than life. I wondered how he and Marilyn would deal with this tragedy. I walked back into our apartment, sank down on the couch, and sobbed.

In the spring of 1966, I also graduated from the University of Minnesota with my teaching degree. We decided to celebrate my graduation at our lake lot one Saturday in June. Sandy planned the food and organized the party. All the food was placed on folding tables on the roof of the boathouse. My entire family and Sandy's was there to help me celebrate an accomplishment I never thought would happen. I wasn't a very good student, and college was a real challenge for me. But, I had made it.

Before we began to eat, Bob prayed for the meal. Dave gave a toast to the second Hall to receive a college degree. We now had two teachers in the family, Dave and me. I received many cards and words of encouragement from everyone. After eating a delicious meal and cleaning up, we got into our swimming suits. We walked over to our lot across the road to enjoy the water and our beach. We spread out our blankets and enjoyed the afternoon in the sun. It was a beautiful day.

"Life is good, isn't it, Mom?" I said sitting down next to Mom on a blanket.

"Yes it is, Son. Congratulations on becoming a teacher."

"Thanks, but I don't think I would have made it without Sandy. She was my inspiration and support."

"Sandy is an outstanding person," Mom said. "You chose a good wife. She is beautiful and smart too. You are so fortunate to have her by your side."

"Can you believe we own this beautiful spot?"

"You boys did well. Your dad would have loved it up here."

"Thanks, Mom, for your selfless life. You rebounded after Dad's death and did a great job with us five younger boys. Somehow, your love and faith in us helped keep us on the straight and narrow and become decent young men."

"It was the Lord who provided, Tom!"

"I know, Mom. Your faith in God is incredible."

I noticed Sandy standing by the birch tree. I walked over and gave her a hug.

"Thanks, Hon," I said to her. "What a great idea to celebrate my graduation at the lake!"

"I know you love it up here, Tommy."

"Sandy, I feel so alive. I'm ready to begin my career and become an adult."

"You are an adult, Tom! You're twenty-four years old."

"You know what I mean. It's time to grow up, become a man, and make some kind of contribution."

"We will have a great future together," Sandy said. "I'm glad you can celebrate with those you love most."

"I'm going to talk to Dave," I stated. "I'll see you later, Babe."

I strolled over to where Dave was sitting under a birch tree next to the shoreline.

"It's a beautiful day, isn't it, Dave?"

"Yes, it is. Look at that clear blue sky next to the deep blue waters of our lake."

"Are you going in for a swim?" I asked.

"In a little bit. Right now, I just want to relax."

"Thanks for your leadership and vision to have a lake home for us," I said. "We couldn't have done this without you. We just have a boathouse now, but some day we'll build a nice cabin too."

"I know we will," he replied. "I'll take the leadership in building our cabin on the back bay, but this will become your job when we decide to build over here."

"I don't think so, Dave. You're the firstborn and the natural leader. I could never take your place."

"Leadership is a great responsibility. It's also a lot of work. I'll do my part, but believe me, when the time comes, you'll have to take the reins."

I didn't like what Dave was telling me and never dreamed it would happen the way he predicted. However, I would never underestimate my big brother.

My four younger brothers were taking turns water skiing. They were all very good skiers and really fun to watch. Bob came in after a ski run, dried himself off, and sat on a blanket on the beach. I walked over and sat beside him.

"What's happening, Bob?" I questioned.

"Oh, not much. That ski run really felt good. Congratulation on your college degree."

"Yeah, thanks. You are the smart one, Bob, and I'm sure you will get many degrees."

"I want to finish college and go to seminary," he said looking out at the lake.

"That's great! You'll make Mom proud. Are you and Jeannie serious?"

"She could be the one. I'm just not sure yet. We'll just have to see how things work out," Bob pondered.

"Can you believe we own this beautiful spot?"

"It's amazing, Tom. It is so quiet and peaceful up here. Sometimes, I have to pinch myself to believe it is really ours."

"Can you visualize a cabin here someday?" I asked.

"I know it will happen someday, but right now, I can't imagine what kind of home we will build on this lot. I guess we can't put the cart before the horse. We need to build a cabin on the other lot first before we can think of having something on this side of the lake," responded Bob.

"It sure was a good move to sell our one lot and buy this one. We all love the water so much, and this beach is unbelievable."

"Yes, Tommy. Where else can you walk into the water up to your neck, look down, and clearly see your toes?"

"I don't know what this place will mean to us in the future, but we sure are off to a good start," I replied.

I was getting warm, so I ran into the lake. I dove underwater and swam a few strokes. When I came up for air, I almost knocked Don over.

"Hey, Don, thanks for the nice card you gave me."

"No problem, Tom."

"How are you doing?" I asked.

"I'm having a great time," he said shaking the water out of his hair.

"You sure have put in a lot of work up here," I stated. "I couldn't believe how you laid those blocks in the boathouse."

"Yeah, I like to work with my hands."

"I appreciate all your help clearing out the land and helping to establish a nice lawn on the other side," I told him.

"It's weird, Tom, but when I work up here, it doesn't seem like work. It is just relaxing, even when we're working hard."

Just then, Jon beached the boat and sat on the beach next to his girlfriend, Janet. I came out of the water, dried myself off, and sat next to them.

"How is the boat running, Jon?"

"It's running fine, but I think we need a bigger motor. This one doesn't have enough power."

"I think you're right. We'll have to discuss that with Dave. I already see a role that you will play up here, Jon."

"What's that?" Jon asked.

"The amount of time you spend fixing things tells me you will be the mechanical one who will do the fixing up here."

"Could be. I don't mind getting my hands dirty. We'll see," Jon responded.

"What do you think, Janet?" I asked.

"Yes, Jon does like to fix things, so I can see him playing that role."

"What a great graduation party! I can't think of a better place I would like to be."

"You and Dave have got your degrees," Jon stated. "Now, we'll all just have to follow suit."

"Remember how much we loved visiting Uncle Auggie at Leech Lake? Then, we went to Keith's cabin, and Dave got the idea of having one of our own," I reminisced.

"Which you almost blew when you took the money out of the box," Jon remembered.

"Some things are just better forgotten."

"You're right, Tommy. Now, we have a place of our own. Who would have ever believed it?"

"This is great, Jon. I hope we have this place together forever!"

"So do I, Tom. So do I!"

I finally got a chance to talk to Steve towards the end of the afternoon.

"How was the water skiing, Steve?" I questioned.

"I love to water ski. I could ski all day."

"I know you could. Are you having a good time?"

"How could you not have a good time up here, Tom?"

"Yeah, I hear you! This is a place I'll never get tired of," I responded.

"Congratulations on graduating from college."

"Thanks. I signed a contract and will be teaching in California next year. I'm excited about that, but I will miss seeing you play hockey your senior year. You sure had a great junior year, Steve!"

"I'll write you and let you know how things are going," Steve offered.

"I'd like that. I don't know how it will go for me out there, but it will be a challenge. I just hope I'm up for it, that's all."

"You'll do great, Tommy. I'm not worried about you. I will miss seeing you though," Steve replied.

"Yeah, and I'll miss you. We've had some great times together."

I had a great time with my family and Sandy's celebrating my college graduation. It was a great weekend and one I would think about often during our first few weeks in California.

That summer, I worked very hard loading trucks at Consolidated Freightways. The job paid well, and the money would come in handy as we began our new life in California. Before we headed for California, I called Dave.

"I will be leaving for California in a couple of weeks to begin my teaching career," I told him. "I was wondering if I could come over and talk to you before I leave."

"Sure, Tom. Come on over tonight. I'll have Marilyn put on a pot of coffee."

Dave, Marilyn, and their two sons Danny and Doug had moved to a beautiful home in Columbia Heights, which is a northeast suburb of Minneapolis. Dave was teaching at Edison High School. I needed his counsel, so I was eager to talk to him. That evening, Dave and I sat in his living room and discussed my plans.

"How long do you plan to live in California, Tom?" asked Dave as he took a sip of his very hot coffee.

"I really don't know," I replied sitting in a chair across the room. "It depends on how well everything goes with my teaching career."

"Do you see this as a permanent move?"

"I've lived my whole life in Minneapolis, Dave. I just don't want to say I never tried anything else. I didn't have a great student teaching experience, so I don't even know if I will stay in education. I love working with kids, but teaching is still a question mark. I've graduated with a four year degree in education, so at least I need to give it a try," I replied.

"It takes a while to become a good teacher, Tommy. I hope you at least give it a good shot."

"I will, Dave, but there is this fear of the unknown that I struggle with."

"With your background in sports, your job as a park instructor, and growing up in a large family, I think you have the tools to become a great teacher."

"Thanks, Dave. In my heart I really want to make this work."

"Do you still want to be a part of the cabin, Tom?" Dave asked. "You won't be using it much living in California."

"Yes, Dave, I want to be a part of the cabin no matter where I live. We've gone through so much together as a family. This project is something I want to be a part of the rest of my life, no matter where I live."

"We have the boathouse built now, so we have a place to sleep when we go up there. However, Tom, I want to build a cabin very soon."

"As you know, Dave, a teacher has his summers off. If you begin building, Sandy and I could come home and help. We will also keep paying our monthly share. Our check will come to you every month when I am gone."

"I'm glad you want to continue to be a part of our lake project," Dave said. "It just wouldn't be the same without you, Tommy."

"Thanks, Dave. I appreciate your leadership in this project. You are the one that made this all happen. It began with Dad's dream, our trip to Keith's parents' cabin, your vision, the saving of our coins, and finally the purchase of our two lots."

"Now, we've cleared the land, and we have a nice lawn, a boathouse, a dock, a boat, and a place that is all ours," added Dave.

"Well, I have to leave now," I said getting up from my chair. "I still have one week of loading trucks at Consolidated Freight Way Trucking. It has been a good paying summer job, but I will be glad to be working with my mind instead of my back. How's Danny doing?"

"The cancer is in remission, and he seems to be doing well right now. I hope it lasts for a while. He seems to be handling everything all right."

"Please keep me posted on his progress. I will pray for him every day."

"Thanks, Tom. We'll keep you informed as to how he is doing. It is tough to see my son struggle with this dreaded disease."

"I know, Dave. I know how much you love him."

"Thanks for asking about Danny. It is sometimes very heavy on my heart."

"I know, Dave, and I'm hurting too."

"Have a good trip out West. I hope all goes well," replied Dave as we headed towards the door.

"Thank Marilyn for the coffee and the hospitality. I hope you can come out for a visit some time. Your boys would love to see Disneyland."

I climbed into my car and headed for home.

A couple weeks later, Sandy and I drove to California. We found an apartment just two blocks from the very blue Pacific Ocean. I had never seen the ocean before. Now, this incredible sight loomed before me from my bedroom window. In the early morning, we could hear the waves breaking against the shoreline. It was soothing. We even had palm trees on our front lawn.

I struggled for the first three months in California. Teaching my own classroom was a challenge and proved to be very difficult. After Christmas vacation, my teaching took a turn for the better. I worked with Bill, another first year teacher from Long Beach, California. He and I became good buddies. He encouraged and supported me in my teaching. At the end of my first year, I had fallen in love with my students. I didn't want the year to be over. It was difficult to say good-bye to my first class that summer. I decided that teaching would be my lifelong career and, hopefully, my passion. I knew, however, there was much work to be done before I could consider myself a good teacher.

I also struggled with homesickness at first. I missed my mom and brothers. I didn't like being on the outside and not knowing many people. Fortunately, I did have a close friend from Minneapolis who lived in our apartment complex. His name was Bob Larson, and he was a physics teacher at the high school in our district. He and his wife, Lynn, became good friends of ours. Sandy's sister, Lucy, also lived nearby.

Sandy and I continued to pray for Danny almost daily. I was hoping God would perform a miracle and heal him from his leukemia. Unfortunately, that was not His plan. One June evening in 1967, the phone rang. I answered it.

"Hello, Tom, this is Dave. I wanted to tell you that we lost Danny today. He died peacefully."

"That's awful, Dave!" I said with tears filling my eyes. "How are you and Marilyn doing?"

"We are both very sad, Tom. He was our first-born. You know how I feel about firstborns."

"Yes, I know, Dave. How will you carry on after the loss of your son?"

"Tom, nothing materially matters to me anymore. My car, my home, and even our lake are not important to me. I really don't know how to answer that question, Tom. But, I'm sure there will be a change in my life."

"You will be in my prayers, Dave," I said. "Please call me and tell me about the funeral. I'm so sorry you lost your boy, but we will see him again in heaven."

"Yes, I know that, Tom. It's the only hope we have."

When I hung up the phone, sadness filled my heart. Sandy and I didn't have any children yet, and I could only imagine how it felt to lose a child. My heart went out to Dave and Marilyn.

Dave's life drastically changed after the death of his son. He totally committed his life to Christ and began to walk with the Lord and study the Bible. He taught a Sunday school class at his church. God was constantly on his mind and heart, and Dave spoke of God often. He became the spiritual head of his home. His whole life changed, and he became a strong follower of Christ. This change in my brother was incredible, and it would have a strong effect on my life in the years to come.

BUILDING OUR FIRST CABIN

Early in the summer of 1968, Dave called with good news.

"Tommy, we are going to begin building our cabin this summer," he announced excitedly. "We are going to build one with a post and beam construction. It will have a flat roof and overlook the lake. We'll have an incredible view of the bay."

"When are you beginning construction?" I questioned.

"We will begin in August."

"I'm taking a summer school class working on my master's degree. However, the class will be over in July. Maybe Sandy and I could come home and help with the construction," I said anxious to help.

"That would be great, Tom."

"Sandy is working for the telephone company, but I think she has some vacation time coming. I'll have her check with her boss and get back with you tomorrow."

"Let me know, Tom. We could use your help."

Sandy checked with her boss and was able to get the first two weeks off in August. I called Dave back.

"Dave, Sandy got the first two weeks in August off. We'll be coming home to give you a hand with the cabin," I stated with a huge smile on my face.

"That's great, Tommy, I'll see you in a few weeks. Thanks for joining us."

"You're welcome, Dave. I'll see you soon. I'm really excited about coming home."

Sandy and I made the trip back home in two days. We averaged ninety miles per hour in several states because the speed limit was "reasonable and proper." Our 396 horsepower Chev Impala had no trouble with this drive. However, I was a little sleep weary when we arrived in Minneapolis. As we drove into the city, the familiar surroundings made me feel warm and at home.

"I guess I haven't been in California long enough to call it home yet," I thought to myself.

We drove to Sandy's parents' home and spent the night with them. Harold and Alice Johnson were retired and lived in south Minneapolis. It was good to be with them again.

Sandy and I drove up to our cabin that weekend. My brothers were all there. The lumber had been delivered and stacked in neat piles on our lot. For the foundation, two rows of blocks had already been laid by my brothers along the back side of our cabin and blocks went halfway up on both sides. The front of the cabin would be supported by posts set in concrete footings. These were completed as well.

This weekend, Dave instructed us as we installed the floor joists and nailed down pressed wood for the flooring. When we were finished, the floor was completed and secured firmly to the foundation and the posts. The next part of the project would be the framing. As we all stood in our driveway gazing at our project before going home, we were moved by the fact that our dream was really becoming a reality.

"The construction has begun, and the cabin is in process. It's up to us to complete this project," announced Dave.

"Do you know how to frame up the cabin?" I asked.

"I'll have to do a little more reading and talk to some of my friends," Dave responded with not very much confidence in his voice.

As Sandy and I drove home that evening, I was deep in thought. We really didn't know what we were doing, and I wasn't too sure about how our project would turn out. I asked Sandy for her opinion.

"If my dad and Roy could come up next weekend, they could frame up the cabin," offered Sandy.

Roy was Sandy's sister's husband and my brother-in-law.

"Do they know how to do that?" I asked.

"Absolutely!" Sandy said. "They are both really good builders and put an addition on Roy's home in Golden Valley."

We were staying with Sandy's parents while in Minneapolis. As Harold and I were sitting in his living room the next day, I explained to him what we had accomplished on the cabin so far. I told him we were ready to begin the framing next.

"Maybe Roy and I could help you boys," suggested Harold.

"That would be great," I replied. "We don't know exactly what we are doing. Dave is the leader but has limited knowledge of building himself."

"Let me check with Roy and see if we can't come up this weekend."

The next weekend, Roy, Harold, and I drove up to our lot. My brothers couldn't make it that weekend, so we were the only ones there. As we drove into our lot, we observed the piles of wood and the completed floor. Roy and Harold assessed everything and discussed what we needed to do. I didn't understand what they were talking about and wasn't much help.

Once they decided on a plan of action, the work really began. Roy and Harold framed the side walls by building the sections horizontally on the ground. Once the completed sections were done, we moved them to the side of the floor, raised them up, and braced them so they wouldn't fall. We did this to all of the walls, and then secured everything to the floor. We also framed the inside rooms and placed a huge rough beam between the living room and the kitchen.

At the end of the weekend, our cabin was all framed in and ready for the plywood sheathing, siding, and roof to be constructed. I was so impressed with how much we accomplished and couldn't wait to see my brothers' reaction. I couldn't believe how hard Roy and Harold worked on a project that wasn't even their own. It was amazing.

We loaded up the tools in Harold's car, cleaned up in the lake, and sat down to eat a dinner that Sandy and her mom had put together for us. After we were finished, we sat on some logs and drank coffee.

"Look at our cabin. It's taking shape, and I can finally see what the finished product will look like," I stated with amazement in my eyes.

"It went pretty good," commented Roy. "Framing is actually fun because it goes quickly, and you can really see progress."

"It was a little difficult placing that beam between the kitchen and living room," responded Harold.

"I can't believe the knowledge both of you have," I remarked. "My brothers are really going to be impressed when they come up next weekend!"

"I'm glad we could help, Tom," responded Harold.

"What impresses me most is that you both worked so hard on a project that isn't even yours," I said emphatically. "Even more than that, you seemed to greatly enjoy what you were doing. I learned so much just by watching you two. I hope I can some day help someone like you've helped my family. When this place is completed, I want you to come up and use it often. I thank you with all of my heart for what you both accomplished for my family."

"Tom, we were glad to do this for you and your family. And you are right. We did enjoy this weekend and especially seeing your excitement!" offered Roy.

The next weekend, my brothers and I traveled to the lake to continue working on our cabin. When we turned into our lot, you could see our cabin all framed up. It looked impressive.

"Wow!" shouted Jon as we jumped out of the car. "Who did all that work?"

One by one my brothers expressed amazement as they observed the work Harold, Roy, and I had done. Even Dave was surprised.

"Why didn't you say something about this on the way up, Tom?" expressed Dave.

"I wanted to see your reaction to the work we did last weekend," I replied with a huge smile on my face.

"You guys must have worked hard," commented Steve as he looked at the structure before him.

"Harold and Roy really know what they're doing," I said. "They measured everything twice to make sure it was correct. They discussed what they were going to do and then went at it. We constructed the walls on the ground and then raised them up, braced them, and then secured them to the floor with nails. The tough part was getting the beam between the living room and kitchen to fit."

"They really helped us out, Tom. Make sure you thank them for us," said Dave.

"I already thanked them and told them to come up often."

Dave gave us each jobs to do, and we began to fill in the frame. Some of us worked on the walls while the rest began on the roof. Dave had gotten a great deal on tongue and groove redwood that we would use to build the roof. Jon and I began building the roof while Dave and Don began working on the siding. Steve was the gopher. He kept us supplied with whatever we needed. Jon and I were sitting on the roof and nailing the redwood to the ceiling joists.

"This is beautiful redwood, Tom. Where did Dave get it?" questioned Jon.

"He got a great deal from the lumberyard that is milling up our trees. It is great wood and will last forever," I explained.

"I like the way the tongue just slides into the groves to form a tight fit," expressed Jon as he slid a piece of redwood six feet long and six inches wide into a piece already secured on the roof.

"Yeah, it sure does fit securely," I replied. "After we get this roof nailed down, we'll lay rolls of roofing paper down and seal the seams with caulk. It will really look nice from inside the cabin to see the redwood with the rough beams holding it together."

"I love building, Tommy. It's exciting to see it all come together," offered Jon as he observed all of us brothers working on this project together like a group of busy bees.

Over the next several days, we completed the siding, tar papered the roof, and caulked and sealed the seams so the roof wouldn't leak. Our last outside project was to build a deck facing the lake. We put steps in the middle headed down to the lawn and installed a railing.

The outside of the cabin was now complete. It looked great with its flat overhanging roof and set of four windows facing the lake. The whole cabin blended into our landscape and had a very rustic look. Our boathouse, which was cut into the side of the hill, seemed to blend in nicely as well. I was amazed at what we accomplished with very little knowledge and not a lot of money.

Now, the challenge was to dig a hole for a big septic tank, sink a new well for the cabin, and put in electricity and plumbing. We still had a great deal of work ahead of us. However, all this work would have to wait until the next summer. Our dream was coming even closer to a reality, and we all had a part in making it happen.

Sandy and I drove back to California. We were sad when we left Minneapolis because it was our home. However, I really enjoyed my teaching job, and California was beginning to grow on us. We had no idea what the future would hold.

AN IMPORTANT DECISION

My third year teaching in California was my best year ever. I was especially close to my students, gained confidence as a teacher, and enjoyed team teaching with my friend, Bill. We had developed a following, and many parents requested to have us as their child's teacher. Bill and I were also attending graduate school together at Long Beach State College. We took the same classes and were well on our way to receiving our master's degrees.

Sandy and I loved our church and developed many friendships. We enjoyed going out to dinner and taking small vacations with our young married friends. None of us had children, so we were free to travel. We took several trips to San Diego, San Francisco, Yosemite National Park, and Las Vegas.

One evening, Sandy and I were discussing where we would settle and raise a family. We were ready to begin a family, but Sandy was not pregnant yet.

"How would you like to live in California permanently?" asked Sandy.

"I'm not sure," I responded.

"Don't you think we better decide where we're going to live before we have children," Sandy stated.

"I really enjoy life out here and being so close to the ocean."

"We've become very active in our little church and have developed some close friendships," commented Sandy looking deep into my eyes. "We have some great friends here. Your teaching partner, Bill, and his wife, Peg, have become very special to us. The Logans and the Kobielushes are great people too. I'm not sure I want to move away from them."

"I've enjoyed playing on the church basketball and softball teams. Also, the men's golf club has been great for me."

"Tom, we need to decide what we are going to do in the future. You have three years of teaching under your belt. If you are going to change school districts, now is the time to consider a move."

"Sandy, Minneapolis was our home. Now that we are married, wherever we decide to live will be our home. I think we could be very happy out here. Besides, you like living by your older sister, Lucy."

"You're right, Tom. It has been fun getting together with Lucy. She was gone when I was only three, so I never knew her as a sister. We've had a great time getting to know one another these past three years."

"We'll probably never find a church like ours back in Minneapolis," I added.

"We need to decide if we are going to stay in California. If we do, we need to begin looking for a home," declared Sandy.

"Let's pray about it, sit on it for a couple of weeks, and make the decision later," I suggested.

It's funny how things have a way of working out. I was seriously considering settling in California. We had established ourselves over the past three years. I was close to getting my master's degree which would mean an increase in salary. If Sandy would work for a couple more years, we could save for a home. Then, something happened that would seriously help us with our decision.

Sandy had been out to dinner with her sister, Lucy. After dinner, Sandy came bouncing in the door with a huge smile on her face.

"What are you so happy about?" I questioned.

"Lucy offered me a job!" she beamed.

"What kind of job?"

"Lucy wants me to be her assistant buyer at Bullocks Department Store. Bullocks is an exclusive store in downtown Los Angeles."

"Lucy makes a lot of money as a buyer," I responded. "Her salary is three times what I make, and she gets a huge bonus check at the end of the year."

"Right, Tommy. She is a very successful buyer. She would train me in, and some day I could become a buyer with a huge salary too."

"Is that what you really want to do, Sandy?" I asked.

She stared at me. I wasn't smiling.

"What's the matter, Honey?"

"I don't know. Something just doesn't feel right," I said leaning back in my chair. "When you look down the road, let's say ten years from now, what do you see?"

"I see us happily married with a family and enjoying life."

"Do you see me alone with the kids while you fly off to New York on a buying trip?"

"No, Tom, I see you coming home from work and the kids and I excited to see you. Then, we'll have dinner together and spend time as a family."

"Sandy, we would have more money, but would we really be a family?"

"Tommy, what I really want is to be a mother, a homemaker, and your wife. That's really all I've ever wanted," she said.

"Sandy, we need to have just one career in this family. We will just have to learn to live on my teacher's salary."

"You're right, Tom!" Sandy agreed. "I'll let Lucy know tomorrow that we are not interested."

"Sandy, I know you would be a great buyer! You are intelligent, beautiful, organized, and have great people skills. But, I also know we are going to have great kids someday and you will be a fantastic stay-at-home mother!"

For the next couple of weeks, I wrestled with the idea of settling in California or moving back to Minnesota. I had come to love California. I was becoming a successful teacher, developing a new confidence, and on the verge of earning my master's degree. I wasn't just a Hall anymore. I wasn't just a good hockey player. People enjoyed and accepted me for who I was. I liked being on my own and away from the comfort of my family. On the other hand, my roots were deep in Minnesota. Could I just walk away from my brothers, my mom, and the cabin? I was perplexed. I knew Sandy would support any decision that I would make. It was my decision, but I was drawing a huge blank. I needed a sign or some kind of help. It came to me in an unexpected way.

We were three weeks from completing another school year. Bill and I had become close friends as well as colleagues. We had grown together as teachers. He was a great supporter of mine and a real encouragement to me. Our teaching styles and personalities complemented each other very well. We loved kids and teaching together.

Bill stepped into my room after the kids were excused one day. I was at my desk working on lesson plans.

"Tom, let's go to the teacher's lounge and grab a cup of coffee."

"Sure, Bill," I answered.

We went into the teacher's lounge, grabbed a cup of coffee, and sat in some easy chairs next to one another.

"How was your day?" questioned Bill.

"I had a good day and a very good year as a matter-of-fact. It's been a blast working together."

"Yeah, Tom. I'll never forget these three years with you!"

That comment bothered me. I looked directly into Bill's eyes.

"Do you have something to tell me?" I asked.

"Yes, Tom, I do."

I did not like the sound of that.

"I just signed a contract with Long Beach Unified School District," Bill said.

His statement hit me like a bombshell.

"You're leaving Palos Verdes School District?"

"Yes, Tom. It's just too long a drive. I have a young child, and I can't spend so much time on the road. Besides, that's where I grew up and my home school district."

"Couldn't you have talked it over with me before you made that decision?" I questioned.

"I interviewed for the job yesterday and was offered the job. I discussed it with Peg, and she agreed that this was the right decision for our family."

"What about me?" I asked selfishly. "I don't want to teach without you!"

"You don't need me anymore, Tom. You've established yourself as a great teacher and are going to have a great career. You have become an impact teacher. I can't believe how you've grown these past three years."

"Bill, you've just taken the wind out of my sails. I don't know what to say."

"Be happy for me, Tom. Wish me the best."

"Bill, right now I can only think of myself," I said. "We had such a good thing going together. I just assumed it would always be this way. I just need a little time, that's all. I am happy for you, and I can never repay what you've done for me these past three years. I was only going to teach one year. Now, I've grown to love teaching, and it will be my life's passion. You're a huge part of my success and love for children, Bill. God bless you. Have a great time teaching back in your own home town."

"Hey, we still have three weeks together. Let's give our kids and this community something they will remember for a long time."

That evening, I drove home along the Pacific coastline with the magnificent blue ocean on my left and gorgeous homes on my right. My heart was heavy. I loved Bill Spivey and just couldn't imagine teaching without him.

I strolled up to our apartment and flopped down into our swivel rocker. I sat there for a long period of time quite dejected. I heard the door slam. Sandy walked in and took one look at me.

"What is wrong, Tom?"

She could read me like an open book.

"Bill's not teaching at Vista Grande next year," I said.

"Now, I understand."

"Sandy, I need Bill. I don't think I can teach without him."

"Yes you can, Tommy. You are a great teacher and have a huge heart for kids."

"I want to go home, Sandy. Are you okay with that?"

"Are you sure?" questioned Sandy.

"Yes, I'm sure!"

"Well then, I'm fine with that!"

That evening I gave my big brother, Dave, a call. He was teaching at Irondale High School in the Mounds View School District.

"Hello, Dave."

"Hey, Tommy. What's up?"

"Are there any openings in your school district for a fifth grade teacher?"

"Wow! You don't beat around the bush, do you? Well, I don't know. Do you want me to do some checking?"

"Yes, Dave, I'd really appreciate that. Sandy and I would like to come home, and it would be nice if there was a job waiting for me."

"I'll see what I can do and give you a call tomorrow," Dave offered.

The next evening after supper, the phone rang. I jumped up from the couch and answered it.

"Hi, Dave. What's happening?" I asked.

"There's a contract in the mail. The job is yours if you want it."

"Wow! You don't waste any time, do you? How did you pull that off?"

"Networking, Tom. It's all about who you know. The personnel director is a friend of mine. I told him I had a brother teaching in California. I said you have been teaching for three years and love kids. He said, 'That's all I need to know. If he loves kids and is your brother, I want him in our district. Give me his address, and I'll send him a contract.' The contract is on its way."

"That is amazing, Dave. I owe you one big time!"

"You owe me nothing, Tom. I'm thrilled that we will be teaching in the same school district together. You'll be teaching at Pike Lake Elementary School. Your students will feed into my high school, so it should be exciting."

"I'll see you in a few weeks, Dave. I can't wait to tell Sandy. By the way, how's the cabin coming?"

"It's all wired now. Bob and I did that project. Jon and I installed the plumbing. Don did a great job with the inside walls of the living room. He used the wood we had milled up, so we have beautiful natural walls of oak, birch, and cherry wood. It looks great, Tom! It's all ready and waiting for your enjoyment."

The next day, I flew into Bill's room. He saw the excitement in my face.

"What are you so excited about?" Bill inquired.

"Vista Grande is history for me too, partner."

"What happened?" Bill asked with a curious expression on his face.

"I called my brother and told him I wanted to come home. He called me back last night and said,

'There is a contract in the mail.' No interview, no questions asked, nothing but a contract," I stated still in disbelief.

"Wow! Someone must sure trust your brother's opinion. They don't know it now, but they'll soon find out it was the best decision that district has ever made. You're going to have a fabulous career, Tom, and I'm happy for you."

"You probably don't realize what your decision to teach in Long Beach did for me, Bill. I have been wrestling with the decision about where to settle down and have a family. I was seriously considering staying right here in California. Your decision made my decision a lot easier. God wants me back home, and he wants you in Long Beach. We just needed this season together. I'll never forget you, Bill, or the three years we've spent on this hill. I've got a feeling we'll be in touch for the rest of our lives."

"I have that same feeling, Tom."

Sandy and I couldn't leave for Minnesota until I finished a graduate summer school course that was designed to help me write my master's thesis. The course took place in June and most of July. When the course was completed, I had the first two chapters of my thesis written. I met with my advisor, Dr. Young, and he agreed to let me finish my thesis by correspondence from Minnesota. I was so grateful he would continue to be my advisor and let me do that.

Sandy and I also had to tell our very close friends from church that we were moving back to Minnesota.

They were sad. None of us had children, and we had spent a lot of time together. They suggested we all take a mini vacation to Yosemite National Park together before we left. That was a great way to say good-bye to our close friends. We had a great time camping together under the stars. The giant waterfall was spectacular and unlike anything I had ever seen. The giant redwood trees had dropped their needles and made our camping spot very comfortable. Our last night, we went out for dinner.

"I have an announcement," I said standing up at the table.

"What is it, Tom?" questioned my good friend, Joe.

"It's a boy, said I. It's a girl, said she. No matter what they say, the rabbit don't lie," I stated and sat back down.

There was about ten seconds of silence, and then the girls started screaming.

"Oh, my gosh!" cried Sharon. "Sandy's pregnant!"

Everyone got up, gave Sandy a hug, and shook my hand. We were the first ones in our group to announce that we were going to have a baby.

"Our due date is the end of December. We'll be back in Minnesota, so we'll call and send you pictures," I announced.

When we went to church the next Sunday, everyone had heard the news. The women there had a baby shower for Sandy before we left, and we received many special gifts for our first child.

Toward the end of July, Sandy and I sold most of our furniture and shipped some things to Sandy's parents' house. We packed up our car and headed for home. As we drove out of Los Angeles, I glanced back. Tears began sliding down my cheeks.

"What's the matter, Honey?" Sandy asked as she looked at my face.

"I can't believe the feelings I'm having and the pit in my stomach."

"I know, Tom. We established ourselves out here on the West Coast. We're leaving behind many wonderful friends," responded Sandy.

"I guess home is wherever we decide to live, Sandy. But, I feel almost as bad as I did when we left Minneapolis," I replied.

On our drive back home, our conversation and thoughts were concentrated on the past three years. We came out to California as strangers and began our careers, made friends, found a church, and grew closer to each other. It was satisfying and yet sad to leave this place we had come to love. However, I knew in my heart I wanted to be back home with my brothers and the cabin.

BACK HOME

When Sandy and I arrived back in Minneapolis, I was positive we had made the right decision. It felt so good to be home again. Sandy's parents greeted us warmly after our three day journey from California. Our 1966 Impala had performed great on the highway even though overloaded with all our belongings. Sandy's parents allowed us to stay in their home until we found an apartment. We enjoyed that time with them.

We soon found a really nice apartment in Brooklyn Center. It was just a fifteen minute drive across Interstate 694 to New Brighton and the school where I would be working. After moving into our two bedroom apartment, we made the drive to New Brighton to investigate my new school. It was a fairly new building with a large playground area. We parked in the front lot, got out of the car, and walked around.

"Sandy, this looks like a great place to teach," I stated.

We walked around the entire building. It was a typical "L" shaped school building with a flat roof, many windows, and numerous classrooms. There was a large grassy area, a small sandy playground area, and a park next to the school. The park had a baseball field and small building. There were wooded areas next to the school and new homes around the perimeter of the playground.

"Let's drive around the area and see what the homes look like, Sandy," I suggested.

We strolled back to the parking lot, hopped in our car, and drove around the area. We noticed attractive homes with well kept lawns. There were two lakes fairly close to the school surrounded by beautiful homes.

"This looks like a lovely neighborhood, Tom," offered Sandy.

"I'd say upper middle class by observing these homes," I responded. "I don't think we'll ever be able to afford a home in this area on my teacher's salary."

"We can't really think of buying a home yet, Tom. I don't have a job, and we'll just have to stay in our apartment until we can save for a down payment."

"Sandy, I don't want you to go to work now that we're having a baby," I stated.

"We'll just have to see how our budget works out when you get your first check. I would really like to stay home if it is at all possible."

Our small amount of furniture and boxes arrived from California. We had to buy a new couch, some chairs, and a bedroom set. It was fun arranging everything in our new apartment. After we had gotten settled, I was sitting in the living room one evening when the phone rang. It was Dave.

"Hi, Tom. What do you have going this weekend?" he asked.

"Nothing really. It will be a week before workshop begins, so I'm just kind of taking it easy," I responded.

"Do you want to go to the cabin this weekend?"

"Sandy, do you want to go to the cabin this weekend? Dave's on the phone and wants to know if we can come up," I shouted to Sandy, who was in the bathroom.

"Sure, Tom, we can do that."

"Yeah, Dave, we can come up," I said turning back to the phone. "Who will be there?"

"Everyone's coming. Marilyn and me, Bob and Jeannie, Jon and Janet, Don and Joy, and Steve and his girlfriend, Kathy, will all be there."

"Wow. We're all married now except Steve. It will be great to all be together."

That weekend, Sandy and I drove up to our cabin on Friday night. I was anxious to see all the work that had been done. We were the first ones to arrive. As we drove into our lot, I noticed our rustic cabin nestled between the trees. It looked fantastic!

Before we unloaded the car, Sandy and I decided to look around. We unlocked the back door, walked into the kitchen, and gazed at the inside of our cabin. A large table sat off to the right side in front of the windows in the kitchen. Dave had put the top of the table together in his wood shop at school. He had glued together pieces of birch and oak from trees on our lot and stained them a blond color. It was sitting on top of an antique barrel and looked great. A sink sat against the wall on our left with the stove next to it. The refrigerator was in front of us against a wall that went about a third of the way across our living room.

As we crossed into the living room under the huge beam Roy, Harold, and I had hung, I immediately noticed the beautiful walls Don had constructed. He had done a great job. The oak, birch, and cherry wood were left their natural color. The redwood ceiling and exposed rough beams were also their natural color. This created a really warm atmosphere. The living room wall separating the kitchen was covered with fieldstone. It was well designed and must have been created by a brick layer. In front of the rock wall was a black, free standing, wood burning stove with a chimney stack extending through the roof.

"Look at that beautiful rock wall, Sandy. Someone who knows what they're doing built that," I commented. "I don't know who built it, but I know for sure it wasn't one of my brothers!"

"Wow!" exclaimed Sandy. "This cabin is beautiful and has such a warm natural feeling to it."

We walked into a small hallway where a doorway opened to a small bathroom. It contained a sink, a toilet, and shower stall. We came out of the bathroom and noticed two more doorways leading to two good sized bedrooms. They were carpeted with different colored carpet samples sewn together. It looked rustic and attractive. There were two double beds in one bedroom, and a double bed, bunk bed, and crib in the other one.

"I guess my brothers and their wives have been busy," I stated. "Everything looks great. Our family has a cabin, and it will be our little retreat as we all grow and have children."

Just then, some headlights shone through the bedroom windows.

"It looks like we have company," I offered.

Sandy and I went outside and greeted Dave, Marilyn, Doug, and their new baby, Jim.

"How was the ride up?" I questioned.

"Not bad. The kids slept all the way up, so that helped."

"Where is everyone going to sleep?" I asked.

"We'll need the bedroom with the crib. You and Sandy and Bob and Jeannie can have the other bedroom. Steve and Kathy can sleep in the kitchen on our folding lawn chairs. They go flat and are comfortable to sleep on with sleeping bags. Jon and Janet can sleep on the hide-a-bed, and Don and Joy can sleep on the floor."

"It's already crowded, Dave. What's going to happen when we all have children?"

"Marilyn and I are planning to buy a small camper. That should give us more room. We'll just have to make do until we can build a cabin on our other lot," replied Dave.

Everyone came up that evening and found a place to sleep. It was crowded, but we still had a blast. When morning arrived, I got up and cleaned up in the bathroom. When I wandered into the kitchen, Sandy and Marilyn were already cooking breakfast.

"Something smells good," I announced as I grabbed a coffee cup from the cupboard.

"Get everyone up, Tom," ordered Sandy. "Breakfast will soon be ready."

"It sure smells good!" I said as I headed for the bedrooms.

"We're having scrambled eggs, bacon, toast, and hash browns," called Marilyn.

Everyone was already stirring. I announced that breakfast was almost ready. We all sat around our huge table and enjoyed a great breakfast and good conversation. After breakfast, Jon and I did the dishes. Sandy and Kathy cleaned up the kitchen, and we were ready for the day. I wandered outside with Dave.

"Let me give you a little tour of what we've been doing while you've been in California," Dave said as we headed out into the backyard.

"I would appreciate that. Everything looks great," I responded.

"Do you see that pipe with the tin can on it?" commented Dave. "That marks our septic tank. Hopkins came in, dug a huge hole, buried a tank, and connected it to our cabin. That is where our sewage goes."

"Wow! That must have been some project!"

"It took them about a week to complete it," Dave responded.

We walked to the south side of the cabin. Dave lifted up a plywood board that was lying on the ground. I gazed into a hole and noticed a pump with pipes heading toward our cabin.

"Pete Moser came and put in this well for us. We'll need to build a shed over it this fall," he explained.

Then, we strolled around to the front of our lot. The large Norway pines looked magnificent and stately as they lined the front of our property facing the bay. We walked down the stairs made out of railroad ties cut in half and set into the hill. The beach was still nice and sandy with some vegetation.

"I see our hockey stick dock is still holding up, Dave," I said.

"Yes, Tom. Coaching hockey has had some benefits."

"I like the way you stacked them on their sides and left a small space between each stick to allow the water to run off."

"Yeah, it's pretty unique. I'm sure we have the only hockey stick dock on the lake."

I ambled out onto the dock, which went out about forty feet into the bay. When I glanced into the water, I noticed many sunnies swimming around the dock.

"How's the fishing been, Dave?" I questioned.

"It's kind of funny. Our neighbors go out all day in their boats, and we just fish off this dock and catch many more than they do."

He walked to the side of the dock and lifted up a large fish cage. It had many nice sized sunnies and a few bass in it.

"Someone's been fishing," I stated.

"That would be Jon. He's out at the end of this dock every spare minute he has. He loves to fish, and this would be his catch. These fish will make a nice meal as soon as Jon cleans them," responded Dave.

I walked back off the dock and stood on the shoreline. Our boathouse with its block construction and flat roof was still holding up fine. I gazed further up the hill. My eyes rested on our cabin snuggled amidst the trees. I couldn't believe that we had built this lake home by ourselves. I took a deep breath as I strolled back up the stairs to the cabin. My heart was filled with gratitude. I loved this place.

That evening after supper, we all gathered around the big table and played penny poker. Everyone was enjoying this place we had built. It was a special evening for Sandy and me after being gone for three years.

As we went to bed that evening, I thought about the future. What would my life be like back in Minnesota? How would the birth of our child impact our lives? Would we have a son or a daughter? What would happen when our family began to expand?

What part would this place play in all of our lives? These questions filled my thoughts. Little did I realize what our small investment would mean to our entire family in the future. I drifted off to sleep with a grateful heart. I knew that as a teacher, I would never be able to afford a place like this without the help of my brothers.

That fall, I began my teaching career in Minnesota. I taught fifth grade at Pike Lake Elementary School. I wasn't a rookie anymore, but I was new to the school. I worked closely with three women teachers. In the sixth grade, all the teachers were men. I bonded with them, and we became good friends. I enjoyed teaching but greatly missed Bill, my friend from California. We still maintained contact through letters and phone calls. I was on my own now and had to establish my own style and relate to new colleagues.

Toward the end of October, my brothers and I headed up to our cabin to do some chores and winterize it. We all got very busy during the school year and realized we wouldn't be using our cabin in the winter very often. Bob had moved to St. Louis to go to seminary and was studying to become a pastor. This left five of us brothers to do the chores. When we got up there, we raked leaves and prepared our cabin for a winter rest.

The raking went fairly quickly. We all worked very hard to clean up the lawn. We raked the leaves onto a large sheet, dragged the sheet full of leaves across the road to our empty lot, and deposited them into a large depression. The leaves would decompose over the winter, so we had room in the depression to put many more leaves for years to come. We pulled in our hockey stick dock and stacked the sections on the shoreline. We winterized our boat, put it on the trailer, and wheeled it into our boathouse. Dave and Jon drained the water pipes and the pump and filled the sinks, toilet, and shower pipes with antifreeze. This would turn into a ritual that needed to be done every fall.

I was sure glad I didn't have to do all that work alone. I wondered how single owners accomplished all this work to maintain their cabins. With all five of us brothers working hard together, we also had time to play and have fun. Through this joint venture, my brothers and I became close not only as brothers but as friends.

On New Years Day in 1970, my son, Michael, was born. Sandy went into labor on December 30th, and we were hoping for a tax deduction. However, she was in labor for over thirty-six hours, and the doctor finally delivered our son by a caesarian operation. The long labor was difficult for Sandy, and I was a nervous wreck. However, when I peered through the glass window at Mike, I realized I was staring at a perfect child. He did not have to squeeze through the birth canal.

A defining moment in my life came when I held him for the first time. I really realized I was now a father. My life would be forever changed. I would be responsible for bringing up a young boy. We took

Mike home from the hospital and laid him in a crib in our second bedroom. As I stared down at this young life, so helpless and dependent, I wondered what kind of parents Sandy and I would be. I had no doubt about what kind of mother Sandy would be. Our family would be her life and focus, but my concern was for me. What kind of a father would I be? I thought of my dad. He was a good provider and a strong leader. He loved my mother and gave me security. However, when he died, I barely knew him. He was so busy providing a living that I didn't get to spend much one on one time with him. As I stared down at my young son, I prayed.

"Dear God, help me to get to know my son. Please give me one on one time with him. Help me to teach him to be responsible and kind. May he always know that I would do anything for him, and may he become a solid Christian man. In Jesus' name, Amen!"

I enjoyed my first year at Pike Lake Elementary and was grateful that I had those three wonderful years in California to build on. When school ended that spring, I couldn't wait to get back to our cabin to relax and unwind after giving myself to my students.

THE SEVENTIES

During the seventies, we Hall boys thoroughly enjoyed the cabin. We fished off the dock, swam in the clear blue lake, and water skied behind our Lund aluminum boat powered by a thirty-five horse Mercury motor. We really enjoyed swimming at our sand beach on our empty lot on the big lake. Although we played a lot, we also worked hard to keep both properties up. As we did, our family grew a lot closer.

At the end of each school year, I would spend time at the cabin. I needed to reflect and think about the past school year. I would think about the successes and the failures. I would go through my class list and think of each individual student. I considered what they had learned in fifth grade and thought about their futures. I wondered what I could do better the next year. As I processed, I went for walks, sat on the dock, drank coffee, and talked with Sandy. I needed this time to reflect before I was ready to move on. This became part of my routine during my entire teaching career. I was grateful to have a place to go and some time to consider the past year. Teaching was my passion, and I wanted to be one of the few teachers my students would never forget. Unwinding at the cabin became very important to me.

I have many cabin memories from the seventies that are special to me. One weekend, Jon and I drove up to the cabin alone. All the families stayed home, so we had the cabin to ourselves. We drove into our property, got out of the car, and were going down to the boathouse. The neighbors, who had bought our lot next door, were clearing their land and getting ready to build their cabin. They had a huge German shepherd. The dog must have thought we were invading his territory because he came charging at us with bared teeth and ears laid back. It was an ominous sight, and we both froze. Paralyzed with fear, we found ourselves staring at this beast in front of us who was ready to tear us from limb to limb. We must have had a stand off for about five minutes. The monster wasn't backing down. We looked to the Robans for help, but no one was around.

"What are we going to do?" I whispered to Jon.

"He can't be that mean, can he?"

I stared into the face of the dog, who looked like a wolf ready to tear into its prey.

"He doesn't appear to be too friendly," I responded.

"I'm going to pet him," stated Jon reaching out his hand to the dog.

Just then, the dog lunged at Jon's hand. He drew it back quickly, avoiding the loss of some of his fingers.

"Did you see that, Tommy?"

"Yeah, nice move, little brother. Do you have any more great ideas?"

"Yes! Let's get back to back so he can't charge us and make our way to the flat roof of the boathouse," suggested Jon.

We turned slowly until we were back to back. Then, very slowly and carefully, we inched our way to the top of our boathouse. The vicious creature followed us all the way growling and ready to attack. Finally, we made it to the top of the boathouse. The dog remained on the ground below but with an evil eye on us. The boathouse roof was flat and just slightly elevated above the ground on the backside. From it, we had a bird's eye view of our hockey stick dock and the back bay.

"What do we do now, Tommy?" questioned Jon.

"Your guess is as good as mine."

"This sucks! We can't even come and be on our own property without being attacked," complained Jon.

"It's not the dog's fault, Jon. He thinks we've invaded his territory. He's just protecting his owner."

"Well, we're going to have to talk with Joe Roban and tell him his dog is on our property. And, we don't like being attacked!" insisted Jon.

Just then the dog glanced away. I rushed off the roof and headed down the hill for the boathouse door. Jon hesitated for a little bit and then tried to follow me. However, the dog noticed him and came charging. Jon quickly retreated back to the roof.

I went into the boathouse and got my fishing rod. When I came out and gazed up at Jon, the dog still had him pinned on the roof while totally ignoring me.

"Jon, come down here," I yelled. "There are frogs all over the place. I'm going to catch some and use them as bait to catch some bass."

"Tommy, this dog won't let me off the roof. Come up and help me."

"What can I do? You'll just have to be patient and wait till he goes back home," I said.

Jon tried several times to get off the roof, but each time the German shepherd made him retreat. In the meantime, I caught five or six frogs and placed them in a minnow bucket. I brought them to the end of the dock, hooked one of them in the lips, and cast it into the water. As it was swimming in the water, the frog suddenly disappeared. I let the line go out slowly. The fish thought he had his dinner and swam slowly away. Suddenly, I set the hook, and the fight was on. The bass fought fiercely. The rod bent as the fish struggled to get loose. He lunged into the air shaking violently and trying to get rid of the hook. I played the fish out and brought it up to the dock. Grabbing him under the lip, I took him off the hook and threw him into the fish cage.

Jon was beside himself watching the whole scene.

"Tom, help me get off of this roof. I want to fish with you."

"Sorry, little brother, but I'm having too much fun!"

I was having the time of my life and caught four or five very nice sized bass. I pretty much forgot about my younger brother. After about forty-five minutes and as I was reeling in my line, I noticed Jon standing next to me with his fishing rod and a frog on his hook.

"I hope you didn't catch them all, Tom."

"How did you get off the roof?" I inquired.

"I tried several times, but the dog just wouldn't give up. Finally, I just sat down and waited. After what seem like forever, the dumb dog went home. Now, it's my turn to fish!"

We fished for another hour, and Jon caught some nice bass as well. We cleaned the fish and froze some of them to take home. We cooked up three or four filets by frying them in butter. We had brought up some beans and cole slaw, so we enjoyed a great meal of fresh bass. It was delicious.

The next day, Jon and I talked to Joe Roban and explained the situation. Joe understood and assured us it wouldn't happen again. It didn't. The dog learned his boundaries and became our friend after he got to know us.

Jon and I had a great weekend together. We had a story to share with our brothers and a life-time memory. I'll never forget Jon trying to pet that angry dog. He was lucky to still have all five fingers.

As time went on, my younger brothers began to have children and all our families began to expand. We still worked a little, played a lot, and always enjoyed the setting of our lake home. Sandy and I bought a small tent trailer that we would bring to the cabin when several families came up at the same time. It only had two full size beds on each side. But, it worked for us because our daughter, Katie, born in 1971, and Mike could sleep on one side and Sandy and I on the other. This served as our bedroom, so we wouldn't take up sleeping space in the cabin. We parked our trailer in the backyard a short distance from our cabin's back door. Sandy and I later traded our small tent trailer for a larger pop-up camper with a stove, refrigerator, table, and fold out beds that could sleep six. We would still bring it up when needed. Dave and Marilyn also had a camper which they kept permanently way out in the back of our lot. Their camper was a little smaller than ours, solid, and didn't need any set up. Both campers took pressure off the cabin and freed up the two bedrooms inside for my younger brothers and their families.

An incident happened in 1974 that sent a deep scare into my heart. In the early, early morning, Marilyn came running over to our camper and started banging on our camper door.

"Tom, Tom!" she screamed.

I heard her hysterical cry, jumped out of bed, opened the door, and saw Marilyn crying.

"What's the matter, Marilyn?" I asked.

"Dave's having a seizure, and I can't wake him up!"

"Sandy, wake up my brothers," I ordered as I ran with Marilyn to Dave's camper.

I opened the door and saw Dave lying on the floor shaking uncontrollably. His boys, Doug and Jim, were wide awake and scared.

Jon, Don, and Steve came running out of the cabin. When they arrived at the camper, Dave was still shaking uncontrollably.

"We need to get him out of the trailer," I shouted.

We entered his small camper and tried to move him, but it was impossible. My heart was racing. I thought my brother was dying. Suddenly, Dave stopped shaking and opened his eyes.

"What happened?" he asked.

"You were having a seizure and shaking violently," I responded.

"I don't remember a thing," he answered.

"Dave, we need to get you to a hospital and have a doctor examine you."

"That was really scary," stated Jon.

"I'm going down to see Champlin on the point," I said. "They are permanent residents here and probably know the best hospital around here."

Dave was now sitting on his bed with everyone around him. Doug and Jim were taken into the cabin.

I ran down to Champlin's A framed home and pounded on the door. Mr. Champlin came to the door.

"What's the matter, Tom? You looked like you've seen a ghost!"

"It's my brother, Mr. Champlin. He had a seizure, and I thought he was dying. We need to get him to a hospital and have a doctor examine him."

"How's he doing now?"

"He's sitting up in his bed and doesn't remember a thing. My brothers and I tried to move him but couldn't get him out the trailer door. Finally, he stopped shaking and came to."

"I'll get dressed and come down in my SUV. We'll take him to the hospital in Rice Lake. My doctor is there. He's a good man and will check Dave out thoroughly."

I went back to our cabin. Dave was still sitting on his bed.

"Can you get dressed, Dave? Champlin is coming to take you to the hospital in Rice Lake."

"Is that necessary, Tommy? I feel better now."

"Yes, it is, Dave. You gave us all a scare. You've never had a seizure before. We need to get to the bottom of this."

"I guess you're right. Shut the door, and I'll get dressed."

"Marilyn, you and I will ride with Mr. Champlin," I said. "You might want to take your purse because they'll probably ask about your insurance."

"Yes, Tom. That's a good idea."

Mr. Champlin quickly came to our aid, and we drove to the hospital in Rice Lake. They wanted to keep Dave overnight. Marilyn filled out some forms, and Mr. Champlin drove us back to the cabin.

"Thanks for your support," I said gratefully as he dropped Marilyn and me off at our driveway. "I'm glad they're keeping him overnight. They will give him a thorough examination to try to get to the bottom of this."

"Yes, thanks for all your help!" called Marilyn.

We walked toward the cabin. When we walked in, everyone stared at us with concerned faces.

"They're going to keep Dave overnight," I stated.

Marilyn sat down on the couch next to Sandy. She started crying.

"It will be all right," stated Sandy reassuringly.

"Dave's always been so strong and in control," she cried. "It's hard to see him become so helpless."

"The doctor will check him thoroughly. I'm sure they will discover what happened and be able to treat the problem," said Sandy as she put her arm around Marilyn.

The next morning after breakfast, Marilyn and I drove back to Rice Lake and arrived there about noon. We inquired about Dave's location and headed toward his room. We walked into his room. He had a tray on his bed and was eating lunch. Marilyn went to his bedside and gave him a hug.

"How are you this morning, Dave?" she questioned.

"The doctor gave me a series of tests this morning. So far, they can't seem to find out what triggered the seizure, especially since it has never happened before. I feel great today. They said I can go home with you. They need to examine some blood tests and will mail me the results. So, as soon as I'm finished eating, we can check out of this place."

We drove back to the cabin that afternoon. There wasn't much conversation in the car. Dave received a letter from the hospital saying that nothing seemed to show up in the tests. It was just something unexplainable that happened. I'll never forget that episode and wondered what it was that triggered his seizure. I would discover my answer in a couple of years.

We had gotten to know our neighbors. We especially enjoyed Harold Hassing, who lived right next door. He and his wife, Mary, had a young child who was autistic. Her name was Anne Marie. I often talked with Harold and asked him questions about building and projects. He had every tool in the world, and whenever we were fixing something, Harold always helped us out. He and his wife used to make homemade wine out of dandelions. He once gave me a glass, and it didn't taste too bad.

One day I noticed several children playing with Anne Marie in their backyard. I saw Harold standing beside his shed, and I approached him.

"Hi, Harold. Are you having a party?"

"These kids are involved in Special Olympics," he said. "They had some events in Spooner, and we invited them to join us at our cabin for the day."

"That's cool, Harold. It looks like they're having a great time."

"Yes, they are, Tom. It's good to see Anne Marie interacting with her friends."

"I'll bet it is, Harold."

These special children were clearly having a great time as Harold and Mary fed and entertained them. As I was walking back to the cabin, I saw Jon standing by our property line watching these children. Just then, one of the young boys spotted Jon. He was tall and must have been around fifteen years of age. He made a beeline toward my brother, who was looking in his direction. Jon noticed him coming and glanced to his right and left trying to figure out where this young boy was headed. Suddenly, Jon realized that he was the target. Jon braced himself. The boy jumped up on him, threw his arms around his neck, wrapped his legs around his waist, and planted a big kiss on his lips.

"Whoa!" Jon yelled as the young boy climbed down off of his body. "He sure is friendly!"

The lad retreated back to Harold's lot when his father called him. Jon was stunned and dumbfounded as he looked around and tried to assess the whole situation. Then, he spotted me doubled over and laughing hysterically.

"Did you see what that kid did to me?" Jon questioned.

"Yes! I can't believe he didn't knock you down."

"I thought he was going to run by me, and then he climbed all over me and kissed me on the lips."

"Jon, I have never seen you so helpless," I laughed. "It was the most hilarious thing I have ever witnessed. I'll never forget the look of desperation on your face as he kissed you!"

"I'll bet you won't," he smirked.

"Was he a good kisser?" I asked.

"Shut up, Tommy!"

Dave was always having us do projects to improve our place. One of our struggles was the well. My brother-in-law, Roy, and I had come up one weekend and built a shed around our well. Sometimes, it wouldn't work, and we were constantly climbing down the hole in the shed to work on it. It was a shallow well, but the water was excellent. The problem was that it sometimes just shut off and had to be repaired. Jon was the one who was usually able to fix the well when it didn't work.

One afternoon, we were having a good time sitting around the big kitchen table after lunch. Jon and Janet, Steve and Kathy, Marilyn and Dave, Don and Joy, and Sandy and I were having much fun teasing and laughing. Sandy got up from the table to go to the bathroom. For some reason, she stopped to look out the front door on her way back to the table when she heard a faint cry by the lake. The cry was muffled and low, and she couldn't make out the sound. As she listened intently, it sounded like a small child's voice. She opened the door and looked toward the lake as the faint sound persisted. Suddenly, horror stuck her face as she realized what was happening.

"Jon! Tom! Quick! Get down to the lake! Chris is in the water. He's behind the boat hanging onto the dock pole. Hurry!" Sandy screamed in a state of panic.

Chris was Jon's second son and only two and a half years old. Jon's face turned white as he jumped up from the table and dashed out the door. Steve and I were right behind him. He flew down the stairs, dashed out on the dock, and jumped into the water. He grabbed his little boy, who was cold and shaking.

"Are you all right, Chris? Don't be afraid. Daddy's got you."

Chris was crying and just clung to his daddy's neck without saying a word. Jon climbed up on the dock with his son clinging to his neck. Tears were running down Jon's face as he walked into the cabin. Janet took her son and hugged and comforted him. She took him into the shower to wash him and warm his little body. Jon and Janet brought Chris into the bedroom and put him to bed. Jon then hit the floor on his knees and began to pray with Janet at his side.

"Dear God, thank you for saving my son. Thank you that Sandy just happened to go through the living room and look out the front door, or did You send her there? I don't know how much longer he could have held on to that dock pole."

Janet and Jon walked back into the kitchen where we all sat sober and quiet.

"He's fine now," Janet assured us.

"How did he get down to the dock? I thought the kids were all in bed napping," asked Sandy.

"I put Eric and Chris to bed," responded Janet. "Chris must have gotten up and walked down to the dock. I think he wanted to play in the boat. He loves the boat. He must have tried to get into the boat and fell into the water."

"It's a miracle Sandy walked through the living room just then and even heard him," I stated.

"The sound was so faint that I barely heard it. But, I intensified my listening and heard the sound again. I wonder how long he had been crying for help," responded Sandy.

"We have to watch our kids all the time, especially when they are this young," I stated.

Mike and Katie were five and three. Jon's two were four and two and a half. Dave's two were six and twelve. And Don's two were four and three. Steve and Kathy hadn't had any children yet. We hadn't really thought about the safety of our children, especially this close to water. We all watched them pretty closely.

"We need to make a rule that no child goes on the dock without a life jacket," I stated.

"Does that include Doug?" questioned Marilyn.

"Doug already is old enough and knows how to swim," I commented, "but all the rest of the children need to obey this rule. We'll need to make that clear to them tomorrow."

That evening as Sandy and I went to bed in our camper, I gazed at my two young children who were sleeping soundly. I wouldn't want to go on living if something happened to one of them. As I lay next to Sandy, I prayed out loud.

"Dear Father, thank you for sparing little Chris's life today. Thank you for sending Sandy by the door. Thank you for giving Chris enough strength to hang on to that pole and cry for help. Thank you for saving his life and giving us parents a wake up call to protect our children up here at the lake. Chris will grow into a fine man some day, and I'm grateful that he is still alive. Please, Father, may You protect our children and draw us close as a family. In Jesus' name, Amen."

Just before I shut my grateful eyes, I heard Sandy whisper a silent amen. My head sank down in my pillow, and I fell fast asleep.

One Sunday afternoon, Steve, Kathy, Sandy, and I decided to go to the little Baptist church in Webster. When we got home and walked into the cabin, Jon, Janet, Dave, and Marilyn were just finishing lunch. They had watched Mike and Katie, our two little children, while we were gone.

"Why don't you and Steve find something to do while Kathy and I fix lunch for you?" Sandy said.

"Let's go down to the dock and take a few casts, Tommy," suggested Steve.

"That sounds like a plan." I responded.

We strolled down to the boathouse, grabbed a rod and reel off the rack by the door, and headed out onto the dock. We hadn't bothered to change clothes yet, so we were both in our Sunday best.

Both rods had artificial lures on them. We walked to the end of the dock and began casting into the bay.

"Well, we're all married now and beginning to have families," I commented.

"Yes, Kathy and I are just in our first year."

"How's it going?"

"Pretty good. I'm still painting and haven't found a good job yet, although painting pays pretty well. Kathy is teaching school, and we decided to wait to begin our family."

"That's a smart idea. You have plenty of time before you need to think about children."

"What's it like being a dad?"

"Once you have children, everything changes. It's harder to focus on each other. Mike and Katie take up most of our time. I need to help Sandy out because she gets very exhausted."

"How do you help her out?" questioned Steve as he threw his bait far out into the water.

"Sandy is a great mom and runs our household. My job is to entertain the children and play with them when she is busy with all her chores."

"Is it hard to discipline the kids?"

"That's an ongoing process. We spank the kids, and it seems to work for us," I stated as I casually cast my gray rapala far into deeper water.

I was reeling it in with my head turned toward Steve when, suddenly, my rod began bending and bouncing.

"Tommy, that looks like a big strike."

"Yeah, and it feels like it too!" I stated.

I was reeling slowly. However, the fish was trying to take my bait to deeper water. The drag was singing.

Steve's eyes got big as he watched me playing the fish.

"What do you think it is?" he asked.

"I hope it's not an eel pout," I remarked as the fish was tiring.

When the fish got about ten feet from the dock, it leapt out of the water and shook violently.

"Holy cow! Steve, it's a huge walleye! I'll never get it up on the dock without a net. I'll just have to beach it," I yelled.

I began walking toward the shoreline. The fish was really putting up a battle.

"Tom, we can mount that beauty and put it on our wall!" screamed Steve as I was making progress toward the shore.

I got it into the shallow waters by the shoreline. The monster was flopping wildly.

"Steve, jump in the water and grab that fish!" I ordered.

"Tommy, I've got my good clothes on!"

"I don't care, Steve. That fish is a trophy. I have to keep the line tight or it will get loose!"

So, Steve jumped into the water, grabbed the fish with both hands, and threw it up on the shore. The fish still had a lot of life in it and was struggling to get back into the lake.

"It gilled me!" he screamed.

"Grab the fish, Steve, before it gets back into the lake!" I yelled.

Instead of grabbing the fish, Steve grabbed the line. The fish snapped the thin line and wiggled back into the water.

"Steve!" I screamed. "You just lost the biggest walleye I have ever seen. Why did you grab the line?"

I was completely out of control yelling at Steve. Suddenly, we saw movement by the shoreline.

"Tommy, the fish is still there!"

This time, leaving caution to the wind, we both pounced on the fish. I got a hold on him, but he was desperately struggling for his freedom. After a short battle, he managed to slip through my grip and escape into the water.

Steve and I were drenched. We just sat in the water staring at each other.

"I can't believe we lost that fish," I moaned. "He was a trophy, and I'll probably never catch a fish that huge in my life."

"I'm sorry, Tommy. I shouldn't have grabbed the line. Just stop yelling at me."

I looked at my little brother, who was drenched and muddy. I fared little better.

Just then, Kathy opened the door.

"Lunch is ready," she yelled.

We hung up the rods and sloshed our way to the cabin. When we walked in the door, Jon took one look at us and broke out laughing.

"Get a load of Steve and Tom," he laughed. "They must have fallen off the dock and landed in the lake."

"If you aren't a sight for sore eyes," Sandy said coming into the living room. "What happened?"

"Don't ask!" responded Steve.

"We had the biggest walleye I have ever seen! We even had it on shore. Steve grabbed the line, and the fish snapped it. Then, it flipped back into the water. I went nuts and was screaming at Steve."

Now, everyone was in the living room listening to our story.

"As I was carrying on with my tirade, we spotted the fish still in the shallow water. We both pounced on the fish, and I got a grip on it. However, it was very powerful and wiggled right through my hands into freedom."

"Wow! That is quite a story you made up," responded Jon.

"You guys need to get out of those wet clothes," ordered Sandy.

Steve and I obediently walked into the bedroom and changed clothes. We sat at our kitchen table and ate a quiet lunch while everyone was laughing at us and teasing us for making up the story. We, however, were too forlorn to even try to defend ourselves.

That summer of 1975 was an excellent year at the cabin. Our families were expanding, and we now had a comfortable place to spend weekends with our extended growing family. In the fall, we raked the leaves, winterized the boat, drained the water, put antifreeze in the water traps, and put the cabin to rest for another year.

DAVE'S STRUGGLE

In the spring of 1976, I walked into our home and greeted Sandy. She gazed deep into my eyes.

"I just received a phone call," she said.

"Who called?" I questioned.

"Marilyn."

I didn't like the sound of Sandy's voice or her body language.

"Dave is sick," Sandy said.

"How sick?"

"They took him to the hospital and ran some tests," responded Sandy.

I can't explain the way I felt, but I knew in my heart it was more than a cold. It was serious.

"The results of the tests were not good. Dave was diagnosed with cancer. They scheduled exploratory surgery to examine the extent of the cancer. When the surgeon went into Dave's body, he discovered a large tumor behind his stomach and in front of his spinal cord. The doctor said the tumor was inoperable because it was so close to vital organs. Dave will undergo chemotherapy to try to reduce the size of the tumor," explained Sandy in a serious tone.

Dave was able to finish out the school year without missing too many days. That summer, we spent a lot of time at the cabin. His cancer seemed to go into remission. Dave and Marilyn had two children, Doug and Jim. Doug was thirteen and Jim was seven. Sandy and I also had two children, Mike and Katie. Mike was six and Katie was four. We enjoyed being at the cabin, and our children loved playing with one another. We didn't work too hard that summer but just enjoyed being together and having fun swimming, fishing, and water skiing.

Even though Dave appeared to be healthy, I knew the cancer was beginning to take its toll. We had many serious talks. On one occasion, we went on a long walk. As we walked, we talked about many things.

"Tom, I took the leadership on building our cabin and boathouse," he stated.

"I know. I am amazed that we pulled it off. We actually built a decent boathouse and cabin. It looks nice, fits well on our lot, and is very comfortable."

"We have a large family and will soon outgrow this small cabin," Dave said with a faraway look in his eyes.

"That's why we bought the other lot, right?"

"That's right, Tommy. There will come a time in the not too distant future that we are going to have to build a much larger cabin to accommodate our growing family."

"I'm sure you are right, Dave," I responded.

"I took the leadership on this project, but you are going to have to be the leader on the next project," he said.

"Dave, I don't want to be the leader. Besides, I don't have the skills or knowledge that you do. You're the firstborn and the natural leader of this family. You have been ever since Dad died."

"Tommy, leadership is a lot of work. It has taken its toll on me. You have to step up to the plate and take your turn."

"I don't want that role, Dave. I can't replace you!"

"I might not be around."

"How's the cancer?"

"It seems to be under control right now, but the tumor hasn't shrunk or gone away. I think my days are numbered."

"Don't say that, Dave. We can't function without you."

"Tom, I'm not afraid to die."

"I know you're not, Dave. You greatly changed after you lost Danny to leukemia. Your faith became strong, and you no longer cared about money or any thing materially."

"Someone has to take the lead up here," Dave said. "It won't just happen."

"We are all adults now, Dave. Just because I'm the next oldest doesn't mean that I'm the next leader."

"It has nothing to do with age, Tommy. Your younger brothers look up to you. They respect you! You are the one to replace me."

"I don't like this conversation, Dave."

"Tom, we have something of great value here. We have a place that could hold our extended family together. You need to do your part!"

"Dave, I've always done my part!"

"I know you have, Tommy, but what I'm asking is that you'll lead your brothers."

"I'll think about it and maybe even consider what you are saying. However, I don't want to cross that bridge until we come to it."

"Fair enough, Tommy. I just want you to know where I'm coming from."

"I know, Dave, but I want you to know that leading this family up here is a role I really don't want to play."

"I hope you change your mind, Tommy, because it's really important to me!"

We had walked down Peninsula Road, made a right on Leef Road, and hiked all the way to County Road A and back again. Neither of us was conscious of where we were going. As our conversation finished, we found ourselves back at our cabin. It was kind of amazing!

That fall Dave began his school year. However, he just had enough energy to teach and crashed when he came home. Finally, the time came when Dave couldn't teach anymore. His body was getting weaker.

Steve and I stopped over to see Dave. Dave was beginning to lose weight, and his stomach was bulging out.

"How's it going, Dave?" I asked as I walked into his room.

"It's a little rough. I don't have enough energy to teach anymore."

"You're not going to die!" stated Steve.

"How do you know, little brother?"

"I found a verse in the Bible that will save you!"

"What verse is that, Steve?" questioned Dave.

"Matthew 21:22 says, 'If you believe, you will receive whatever you ask for in prayer.' The Bible also says, 'If two or more agree on anything and ask in prayer, your request will be granted.' Mark 11:24 says, 'Therefore, I tell you, whatever you ask for in prayer, believe that you have received it, and it will be yours.'"

"That sounds good to me, Steve," responded Dave.

"If we agree that this statement is true, we can pray this prayer together. However, we must believe and not doubt in our heart, or this prayer will not be answered. The key to this prayer is our faith," stated Steve with confidence.

So, in Dave's bedroom, we all agreed that God would heal Dave. We stood on God's word and were confident that our big brother would totally recover. As Steve and I left Dave's house that night, Steve was very firm with me.

"Tom, you cannot doubt. Your faith must be strong. Dave's life depends on that!"

"I believe, Steve!"

"You must believe in Dave's healing and confess with your mouth that he is already healed, Tommy. If you do that, God must heal him because we are just praying back His words," he said emphatically.

"All right, Steve. I believe and will not doubt. I will confess his healing even before I see it."

After that incident, I continued to believe my brother would be healed and confessed verbally that he was already healed. I went over to Dave's house often. We spent time talking at his bedside. He wanted me to read from his Bible, which I did often. As time went on, I noticed my brother getting weaker and weaker. However, I tried to ignore his decline and continued to confess his healing.

This faith stand became more difficult as Dave's health continued to decline. It became more and more difficult to believe in his healing as I watched his life slipping away. It affected my teaching, my family, and me personally. Doubt began attacking my mind, and I continued to try to fight back with belief. Finally, I couldn't stand it any longer. I thought my lack of faith and doubts were killing my brother.

I was home one evening struggling with all of these issues and walked out into my backyard. I shook my fist in the air and screamed.

"Where are You, God! You created the whole universe. I am Your son. I have one little request. Kick the tumor out of my brother's body. That is not hard for You!"

I began crying.

"Why aren't You listening to me? You've never answered my prayers. I'm not praying for myself. I want You to heal my brother."

Then, I lost it.

"God, I hate You! My brother is going to die. It is worthless following You. You don't care!"

I had never been this emotional in my life. I laid on the ground and sobbed my heart out. Suddenly, in my mind, I heard a still, small Voice.

"Just who do you think you are talking to?"

I opened my eyes and looked upward. The Voice spoke again.

"Who does your brother belong to, you or Me?"

I was frightened.

"He belongs to You," I responded.

"That's right, he belongs to Me. When are you going to trust Me? You never have trusted Me!"

I realized for the first time in my life I had never really trusted God. He was right. God was calling me on the carpet. I was shaken and humbled.

"I trust You, God!"

"Then it is My call if I choose to heal him or call him home. I want you to trust Me!"

"You are right!" I said. "Dave belongs to You. You will do what is right. I do trust You. You are the object of my faith. If You call me to do something and I know it's Your voice, I will obey. From this point on in my life, I will trust You!"

As I laid on the ground that dark October evening, I stopped crying. Suddenly, peace came over my body, and I felt relief. My brother's life was not in my hands nor did it depend on my faith. Dave was in God's hands. God revealed Himself to me, and I felt peace.

I don't know how long I laid on the ground. I got up, wiped the tears from my eyes, and went into my house. Sandy was asleep in bed. I slipped in beside her, pulled the covers up to my chin, and fell fast asleep. When I woke up the next morning, I felt refreshed and calm. Something great had happened in my life, and somehow I knew I would never be the same again.

I didn't share this experience with anyone for quite a while. My heavy heart was lifted, and my times with Dave were real and refreshing. Finally, when I was visiting him one evening, I shared this experience with Dave. He listened intently.

"Tom, I'm not afraid to die," he said when I was finished. "I'm only sorry that I won't see my kids grow up. I'm also interested in biblical prophecy. The last days will be exciting."

"Dave, I'll live for both of us."

"Tom, just live your life for God. Don't be bitter after I'm gone. Live your life totally trusting God. That is the best you can do for me."

"I do trust Him, Dave. I trust Him with your life as well as mine."

After that conversation, Dave and I had great fellowship with one another. On one occasion, Dave asked me to pray for him.

"Tom, I believe I am going to die. I would like to talk to my friends before I go."

Dave had six or seven very close friends from his childhood. They had remained friends throughout the years and got together once a month. Marilyn brought Dave to see his friends for the last time. After they were finished talking and laughing together, Dave told them he had something to say.

"Guys, I'm probably not going to make it," he said with conviction in his eyes. "Let me tell you about my faith in God. Jesus was God the Son. He lived a perfect life. He sacrificed his life on the cross, was buried, and rose again. He is alive now and at the right hand of God, and someday He will return and reign with His children. I've repented of my sins, accepted God's grace, and made Him Lord of my life. I believe because I've accepted this gift, I will live with Him forever. I will be in heaven waiting for you. Please receive Jesus as your Savior and join me in heaven."

Dave then looked at Marilyn and asked to be taken home. His friends were stunned and sat in silence. I don't know what impact this incident had on their lives, but it was something Dave absolutely needed to do.

In the first part of December, Marilyn called me. I could tell by her voice that she was very distraught.

"Tom, Dave has fallen, and I can't get him up. Could you come over and help me?"

"Absolutely, Marilyn. I'll be right over."

"Sandy, Dave has fallen, and I need to be there," I stated as I ran out the door.

"I'll pray for you," Sandy responded.

"Dave is very weak," Marilyn said when she answered the door. "I can't take care of him anymore."

I found Dave lying on the floor. My big strong brother looked so weak and helpless.

"Dave, put your arms around my neck," I said. "I'm going to stand up. My legs are strong, but you need to help me as much as you can."

So, Dave put his arms around my neck, I stood up, and he worked with me. We got up and slowly made our way to his bedroom. I helped him get on his bed.

"It doesn't look good, Dave."

"I'm very weak, Tom."

"Dave, you can't stay at home. Marilyn can't care for you any longer. I need to take you to the hospital."

"Tom, if I go to the hospital, I'll never come home again."

"You're right, Dave, you won't. You have to think about your family. They can't care for you any longer."

"Get my boys in here, Tommy."

I walked out of Dave's room and approached Marilyn.

"We need to take Dave to the hospital. You can't go on like this anymore."

"I know, Tom. It's just too hard."

"He wants to talk to his sons."

"Jim is sick, but I'll send Doug in to see his dad," Marilyn responded.

Doug, who was thirteen years old at the time, came into his father's bedroom.

"Doug, Tom is taking me to the hospital. I won't be coming back," Dave said.

Doug just looked at his dad and made no response.

"Tom knows what it's like to grow up without a father. He was about your age when our dad died. If you need support or help, you can always talk to Tom."

I don't know if Doug was in shock or what, but he just wasn't able to respond to his dad. He left the room without saying anything.

"Okay, Tom, I'm ready to go," Dave said.

Marilyn had called Merlin, Dave's friend and neighbor, to help get Dave to the car. When he came into the house, he appeared shook up.

"Hi, Tom. I understand you need some help," Merlin said.

"Yes, Dave is quite weak, and we need to take him to the hospital. I'll need your help to get him to the car."

Merlin and I went into Dave's room.

"Merlin is going to help get you into the car, Dave."

"Thanks, Merlin."

"You're welcome, Dave," Merlin responded.

Dave draped his arms around our shoulders, and we slowly made our way to the car. Marilyn opened the car door, and we slid Dave into the front seat. Dave had trouble sitting upright until

I buckled him in and snapped the seat belt tight. Merlin closed the door, and Marilyn got into the back seat. I jumped into the front seat and propped one hand against Dave and the other hand on the steering wheel. As I pulled out of Dave's driveway, I glanced at Merlin, who was standing and watching us leave. His face was distorted, and tears were freely flowing down his face.

Marilyn had called ahead, so the hospital was prepared for us when we arrived. Marilyn went into the hospital, and an orderly came out with a wheelchair. He placed Dave in the wheelchair and took him into the hospital with Marilyn following. By the time I parked the car, Dave was already settled in a room. Marilyn and I stayed by his bedside for about an hour before we went home.

The next day, I went to the hospital to visit Dave. He was sleeping as I entered his room. I pulled up a chair and sat just staring at his body which was weak and frail. My big, strong, invincible brother was laying in his hospital room dying, and it was killing me!

"Why, Father, is my brother so sick, and I am so healthy? I just don't get it. I'm greatly struggling, and I can't handle this. First, I lose my father, then my nephew Danny, and now Dave. You asked me to trust You, and I do. But, I am hurting so bad, and I need some comfort. Could You please help me?" I prayed.

Tears were freely flowing down my face. As I opened my eyes, I glanced at Dave who was staring at me.

"What's the matter, Tommy?"

"Why do you have to die? Our family needs you. You're the leader and cannot be replaced."

"I'm not afraid to die."

"I know you're not, Dave."

"I don't want you to be bitter or angry. You need to carry on and do the best you can. This is not the end. I'll see you in heaven."

"Dave, we've been through so much. You stepped in when Dad died. You coached us all in hockey. You directed our cabin project which is not completed yet. You even got me my teaching job, and we are colleagues. It's just not fair, Dave."

"I wish I could be around to see the cabin you build on the new lot. I'll bet it will be beautiful," he said with a faraway look in his eye.

"I don't know if I can lead the family the way you did."

"I have faith in you, little brother. You'll be a great leader. I know you will do what you can to keep our family together. Dad would have loved that."

"Greet Dad for me. Tell him we're doing all right. Thank him for the great job he did raising us wild Hall boys."

Just then, my sister walked into the room. I stood up and offered Gwen my chair. She sat down and took Dave's hand.

"It doesn't look good, Dave."

"No, it doesn't, Gwen. I want to apologize for not being the loving brother that you needed and deserved. Will you forgive me?"

"Yes, I will forgive you, but I was no angel either."

"Tom and I just had a nice chat. He needs to take my place with the younger brothers."

"I'm sure Tommy will do just fine, Dave."

"Gwen, I've made my peace with God, and I'm ready to go home," Dave said confidently.

"I'm sure you are," answered Gwen with tears streaming down her face.

"Thanks for being a wonderful sister. You are a great person, and I respect you a lot."

"I respect you too, Dave. You've done well and are a great person as well as an outstanding teacher. I'll see you in the morning," stated Gwen as she got up to leave.

As she glanced back at Dave, she noticed his arms were extended towards her. She moved back to his bed and gave him a long hug and a kiss.

"I'll see you tomorrow," she said.

"No, Gwen, I'll see you in the morning."

As I observed this scene between my brother and sister, I realized that God had answered my prayer. I needed to be comforted, and the scene played out before me in this hospital room had done just that.

Gwen and I walked out to the parking lot together. Both of us were very quiet and deep in thought.

"Gwen, when you and Dave embraced and kissed one another, I was deeply moved. You weren't exactly bosom buddies."

"Tommy, you'll never know how special that was to me. I'll remember that moment for the rest of my life!"

As I got in my car, I knew it was the last time I would ever see my brother on this earth. The tears flowed freely all the way home.

My brother died the next day in the hospital with Marilyn at his side. A funeral was held the next week. We had a reviewal the night before the funeral. People from all walks of life came to pay their last respects to Dave. I especially remember students and hockey players standing at the coffin and staring at his body. I wondered what was going through their young minds. Neighbors from our cabin came to say good-bye to Dave. I knew my brother did not live in vain. He touched many lives. It was a difficult and emotional night for all of us as we interacted with people who were touched by my brother's life.

Dave's pastor, Paul Waite, presided over the funeral the next day. The church was packed with people of all ages. Irondale High School dismissed school at noon, and many students and faculty members attended the funeral. I was sitting with my family in the front row. My brother, Bob, gave a powerful eulogy. At the end of the funeral, the organist passionately played "The King is Coming." It was one of Dave's favorite songs. This song reminded me of the promise we have that Jesus Christ is coming back for His children. I knew this wasn't the last time I would see my brother.

We all grieved in our own way. It is tough to lose a husband, father, brother, friend, and son. Mom took Dave's death especially hard. Life would carry on as time would heal the hurt, but for now, our family had a huge hole in it.

Later that winter, the phone rang. Sandy answered it.

"It's for you, Tom," she said.

"Hey, Tom! This is Bob Kobielush. How are you?" said the voice on the other end of the phone.

"I'm fine," I responded, which was not true.

Bob was a friend I had met while living in California. We had similar backgrounds. His mother had raised five boys without a father as well. We had become good friends at our church in California. Bob was studying to be a minister but really wanted to direct a Christian camp. I remember him saying that some day he would direct a large camp and would have me run it.

"What have you been up to, Tom?" he questioned.

"Just teaching school and doing life," I responded.

"I have a proposition for you," he stated.

"Oh, what's that?"

"I have been directing Trout Lake Camp for the past few years, and I need someone to run my program this summer. How would you like to be my man?"

"Trout Lake, huh? I used to go to Trout Lake Camp as a child. I loved that place!"

"It's a great camp, Tom. It's located in northern Minnesota on the Whitefish Chain."

"Thanks for the offer, Bob, but I don't think so. I lost my brother to cancer last month, and I'm not in very good shape right now. Besides, I really don't know anything about running a camp."

"I'm sorry to hear about your brother. I know you Hall boys are very close. Which brother was it?"

"It was Dave, my oldest brother. I'm kind of struggling with everything right now, Bob. I don't think I have very much to give."

"Tom, this may be a God thing. I have been praying for the right person to be my program coordinator this summer. I know you are a teacher and have your summers off. I was driving down the freeway and glanced over and spotted your house. As I continued down the road, I had a sudden urge to call you. Would you be open to pray about it?"

"Yes, Bob, I'll pray about it, but I think you should continue to look for someone else."

"Okay, Tom. As far as knowing what to do, I could give you a crash course. I know you would do a great job, and I would love to be connected with you again."

"Thanks, Bob. I'm really flattered that you would even consider me. I'm sure it would be a great opportunity. Unfortunately, the timing is not quite the best right now."

"I understand, Tom. It was good talking to you, and I'll be praying for you as you grieve the loss of your brother."

"I really appreciate that!" I said as I hung up the phone.

I walked into the living room where Sandy was sitting reading the newspaper.

"Who were you talking to, Tommy?"

"You won't believe it, Sandy, but that was Bob Kobielush. He offered me a position to direct Trout Lake Bible Camp this summer."

"What did you tell him?" she asked.

"I told him I just lost my brother and was in no shape to direct a camp."

"Are you sure you don't want to do that, Tommy?"

"Sandy, I'm in no shape to direct a camp. That would take a tremendous amount of energy. We would have to shut up our home for the summer and move to the camp. Is that something that you would consider?"

"Maybe," she stated looking me directly in the eyes.

I dropped the conversation and didn't want to discuss it anymore. I was very surprised by Sandy's reaction. I couldn't believe that she would even consider leaving our home and moving to a camp with two small children. I continued doing life by teaching school and trying to be a good husband and father, but Bob's conversation kept ringing in my ears.

"Maybe it's a God thing, Tom. Would you a least pray about it?"

His words wouldn't leave me. So, I began praying and asking God if he wanted me to accept this position. I talked with some of my Christian friends and asked for their prayer support. Finally, one Sunday after church, I talked to my pastor, Paul Bubna.

"Paul, could I meet with you some time next week?" I questioned as I walked out of church shaking his hand.

"Sure, Tom. Is there some sort of problem you are struggling with?"

"Not really. Oh, I'm still hurting and grieving the loss of my brother, but that's not what I want to talk to you about."

"Could you come to the church after work on Tuesday at 4:00 PM?"

"Yes, that would be great. I'll see you then."

That Tuesday after work, I drove straight to the church, which was only a couple blocks from my home. I walked into the church office and was greeted by the church secretary.

"Hi, Tom. Pastor Bubna is expecting you. You can walk right into his office."

As I walked into Paul's office, I thought about this man. He was not only my pastor, but my good friend and mentor. He was about ten years older than me and had five children. We lived in the same neighborhood. We had spent time one on one, and he greatly helped me grow in my Christian faith. I had great respect for him.

"Hi, Tom," he said as he pushed his Bible and sermon notes to the side.

"Hi, Paul. Thanks for seeing me so quickly."

I pulled up a chair in front of his desk and sat down. He gazed at me with puzzled eyes as if he were trying to read any trouble in my body language.

"I have a friend that I met while teaching in California. He is now the director of a big Christian camp in northern Minnesota. He called and asked if I might be interested in directing Trout Lake Camp this summer. I turned him down but have really been struggling with that decision," I stated looking directly into his intent eyes.

"Trout Lake Camp, huh? That's a great camp, Tom. Why did you turn him down?"

"As you know, I just lost my brother and don't feel like I have anything to offer. And beside that, I own a lake home with my brothers. I thought I might just chill out this summer and spend time with my children."

"So, what's the problem, Tom?"

"I don't have peace about that decision."

"Have you discussed it with Sandy?"

"Just briefly. She doesn't seem to be entirely opposed to the idea, which really surprises me."

"Have you prayed about it, Tom?"

"Yes, Paul, and that's why I want to talk to you."

"Go ahead, Tom."

Paul was always direct with me and didn't beat around the bush, which I greatly appreciated.

"Paul, I had an encounter with God during Dave's illness. I was angry and upset that my prayers weren't being heard. The struggle lasted for some time. When it was over, I told God that I would trust Him with not only my brother's life but with everything. I said that if He ever asked me to do anything, I would do it. Now,

He is asking me to direct a large camp. I know nothing about directing a camp, and I'm scared," I said.

Tears were streaming down my face. I didn't try to hide them or wipe them away, nor was I ashamed.

"I can see your struggle!"

"How do you know if God is calling, Paul?"

"You just know. And you know that God is calling you to direct this camp. Don't you, Tom?"

"Yes, I do, but why now, Paul? It's the last thing I want to do!"

"Tom, we've spent time together. You are serious in your Christian faith and your walk with God. It is time! God is calling you off the bench and asking you to play the game. I don't think you can sit on the sidelines any longer, my friend."

"I need prayer support. Will you support me with prayer?"

"Absolutely! Give me specific things to pray about. God is going to use you and your family in a powerful way this summer. I will pray for you every day."

"Thanks, Paul. I already knew the answer, but I needed some confirmation. I know it will not be an easy summer. I will covet your prayers and will keep you posted on a weekly basis with a letter or phone call."

He gave me a huge hug as I left his office. I knew what I needed to do. That evening after I put the kids to bed, I told Sandy about my conversation with Paul. We agreed that the summer would be spent at Trout Lake Camp.

That summer, we packed our car, locked our house, and spent an unbelievable time at Trout Lake Camp. After a couple weeks, I knew I was way over my head and couldn't handle the job. Sandy came to my rescue. She organized a schedule for my day, and we worked together. The Lord did some remarkable things not only with my family, but with the camp as well. I was the up front person who made it happen, and Sandy was my strength behind the scenes. Our gifts blended together, and we were an awesome team. For the first time in my life, I felt like a tool in God's hands.

My family spent two unbelievable summers at this wonderful camp. But, that's another story. I'm only mentioning it here because we were not able to go to our cabin for two summers. After the two years at Trout Lake Camp, it became clear that the Hall family had now outgrown our little cabin. It was time to either build a new one or sell what we had and purchase one already built.

DO WE BUY OR BUILD?

After spending two summers at Trout Lake Camp, I was ready for some relaxation at the cabin with my family again. During the spring, my brothers and I had many discussions about building a new cabin. We couldn't agree. Should we sell our cabin and empty lot and purchase a cabin already built, or should we build one ourselves?

There were six of us on the deed. The five brothers and my sister-in-law, Marilyn, were all co-owners. My brother Bob was living in New York and working as a minister. He couldn't really afford to make payments for the cabin, but we decided that we wanted him to be a part of our cabin even if he couldn't contribute financially.

One weekend, we were all together at the cabin trying to decide what to do, and the discussion got very interesting. It was a Saturday night, and the kids were all down for the night. Kathy had fixed a great dessert, and we were all sitting in the living room.

"We could probably get $30,000 for our cabin and another $30,000 for our lot. We could probably find a cabin big enough for all of us and pay cash for it," I suggested.

"Who's going to pay $30,000 for our cabin?" questioned Marilyn.

"I think I know someone who might be interested," I answered. "He would probably give us our asking price."

"Who is that?" responded Steve after taking a sip of his coffee.

"My friend, Larry Martin, has been interested in purchasing a cabin."

"I really like our lot, Tom," stated Janet, Jon's wife. "It has a beautiful beach and is close to the water. I don't like to have to walk down a huge bank to get to the lake."

"Maybe we should look around and see what's out there before we make our decision," added Marilyn.

"I don't know if we can find a much better lake than ours," threw in Jon. "It has depth and is a good size. The water is clean, and there are plenty of fish. I think we should sell our existing cabin and use the money to build one on the other side."

"Who's going to take the leadership now that Dave's gone?" I questioned.

No one answered that question, but everyone looked at me.

"That's what I thought," I said. "Just because I'm the next oldest doesn't mean that I'm the leader. I don't have the knowledge or skill that Dave had. We are all adults now, and I'm not necessarily the leader, nor do I want to be. I think Jon should be the leader."

"Yeah, right!" stated Janet. "We have four children, and Jon has all kinds of time to build a cabin and support our family. It should be you, Tom. And besides, you're a teacher. You have your summers off."

"Well, I haven't had a summer off yet," I said. "I need to work just to pay the bills. I'm the total bread winner, and teachers aren't exactly paid a high salary."

That evening we went round and round about building or selling our properties and buying something already built. We could not come to a decision and dropped the subject after much discussion. The next weekend, Steve and Kathy were up at the cabin with Sandy and me and our children. Steve and I were sitting on the dock discussing what we should do about the situation.

"I think we should build a new cabin on our lot, Tommy," Steve said.

"Steve, do you know what's involved in building a new home? That's what it would be, a new home. It will have to be big enough for each family to have a bedroom. We're talking five bedrooms and probably two bathrooms. It's a mammoth job, and I would get stuck with carrying the load. Dave talked to me about the stress of building our old cabin, and I don't want that stress in my life right now, Steve."

"No one else will take the leadership, Tommy. You've got to do this for our family."

"No, I don't, Steve. You do it!"

"People wouldn't follow me like they would you, Tom. You know that!"

"Steve, I'm afraid of that much responsibility. I'm not Dave!"

"Let's go to a realtor in Webster and look at some cabins for sale tomorrow. Maybe we'll find something really nice that will solve this problem," suggested Steve.

The next day, Steve and I drove to Webster and searched for a real estate office. Webster is a typical small town in Wisconsin of about 500 people and is located on Highway 35. There is a drive-in restaurant on one side of the town with shops and a couple of gas stations in between. On the main street, there are several small businesses on each side of the road. The cars park perpendicular to the sidewalk facing the shops.

When we were not successful in finding a realtor, we decided to drive to Siren which was just five miles away. We found Lakes Real Estate on the main road. We knew them because we had worked through them to buy our bay properties. We pulled our car into the driveway and entered the office. A pretty young secretary greeted us.

"Can I help you gentlemen?" she asked.

"We're interested in looking at some lakeshore property," I stated.

Just then a gentleman came out of a small office.

"Frank, these young men are interested in looking for some lakeshore property. Can you help them?"

Frank walked over to us and extended his hand.

"Hi, I'm Frank Norman. What did you boys have in mind?" he asked as I shook his hand.

"I'm Tom and this is my brother Steve."

"It's nice to meet you," he said extending his hand to Steve. "Why don't you come into my office, and we'll see what you're interested in."

We followed him into his office and pulled up a couple chairs facing his desk.

"Do you know the area?" questioned Frank.

"We have a place on Sand Lake and have been here for a few years," responded Steve.

"Sand Lake is very choice property. How long have you been there?"

"We bought two lots in 1963 and have built a cabin on the bay side of the peninsula," I stated.

He gazed at us to try and figure out if we were serious buyers.

"Why do you want to look at property if you already have a place on Sand Lake?" asked Frank.

"Actually, we own the cabin with three other families," I said. "We've outgrown our cabin, and we are contemplating selling our cabin and lot in order to buy an existing building that would fit our needs."

Frank showed us several properties, and we decided to examine them personally. He took us to several homes. Some were very exceptional. However, none of the lakes compared to Sand Lake.

The final cabin he showed us was located on Sand Lake on the east side. It had a double garage and a nice big lawn and was a good sized lake home. It was a two story building with a walk-out basement facing the lake. As we walked through the home, we viewed a large brick fireplace, good sized living and dining room, three bedrooms, and a bathroom. We walked downstairs and noticed a large unfinished room with windows in the front facing the lake. The front of the cabin had a smaller lawn with large Norway Pines facing the lake. It was a gorgeous view high above the water. We walked down to the lake on wooden steps made of railroad ties. On the lake there was a dock with a speed boat tied to it. There wasn't much of a shoreline or a beach.

"What are they asking for this place, Frank?" Steve asked as we headed back to our cars.

"Do you like this place?" questioned Frank.

"It's very nice," I responded.

"It's not a cabin. It's a lake home, and the Sawyers live here year around," he said.

"How much are they asking for this place?" Steve questioned again.

"They want $72,000, but I'm sure they will negotiate. Do you want to make an offer?"

"We need to check with our wives, brothers, and sister-in-law before we make an offer, Frank, but we are interested," I said.

We thanked Frank for showing us the homes, hopped into my car, and headed back to our cabin.

"What do you think about that place, Steve?"

"It's very nice, but $72,000 is a lot of money, Tom."

"We could offer $60,000, and see what happens."

"Don't you think everyone should see this place before we make an offer?" offered Steve.

"Yes, I think that would be a good idea. If we could sell our lot and cabin for $60,000, it would be doable. I like the idea of a place already built. I know what a hassle it will be to build our own place."

When we got back to our cabin, we discussed our find with Sandy and Kathy. They said the other owners needed to see the property. The following week, we all went over to look at the Sawyers' lake place. They were home, and we introduced ourselves and asked if we could see their home. We explained we had a cabin on the bay and some property on the west side of the lake on the peninsula.

After we all viewed the property, we had quite a discussion on whether or not to make an offer. My argument was that it was a year around home already built. I said we could finish off the basement and have two more bedrooms. Janet, Jon's wife, was particularly not in favor of purchasing this place.

"If we buy this place, I will not come up here!" she said emphatically.

I was able to convince everyone that $60,000 would be an excellent price and a great investment.

Steve and I contacted Frank the next day and made an offer of $60,000 for the property. Frank delivered the offer to the Sawyers. That week, I got a call from Frank saying the Sawyers were insulted by our low offer and wouldn't consider anything less than $70,000. After contacting all the owners, we decided not to pursue this property.

A few weeks after this incident, we were all up at the cabin sitting around our large homemade table Dave had made. Janet spoke up.

"I contacted Martin Homes," she said. "It's a company that works like Capp Homes. They deliver all the material on a semi trailer and build a stick built home. They will do all the work or only as much as we want them to."

"I've heard of Capp Homes," stated Don. "They build nice places."

Janet pulled out a booklet containing many floor plans.

"I've examined many of the homes and found one that I thought would work for us," she said thumbing through the booklet.

She came to a plan for a rambler that looked interesting.

"This floor plan would work for us," she said. "The problem is that it only has three bedrooms, but we could extend the length and add two more which would give us five."

"I like the front deck," I said as I examined the blueprint.

"The kitchen extending into the dining room is a good idea for an eating area," offered Sandy.

"Our large table would fit into the dining room, so there would be plenty of room," added Marilyn.

"There will be two bedrooms on the back side of the house," Janet pointed out. "These bedrooms will be larger than the three facing the lake."

"The larger families can have the bigger bedrooms, and those who have smaller families can have the lake view," I suggested.

I was amazed because we all seemed to be in agreement. Janet agreed to pursue the price and research how to get everything in motion. I agreed to contact my friend Larry to see if he was interested in buying our cabin. We suddenly all came together and decided to build a cabin on our empty lot. It seemed to be the right decision. However, I knew a tremendous amount of work needed to be done to complete this task that we were about to embark on.

Sandy and I stayed at the cabin while my brothers all went home on Sunday night. After the kids went to bed, I wandered over to our empty lot and sat on the small bank overlooking the lake. There was a full moon shining brightly in the night sky and leaving its beam on the clear water. It was a warm summer night with a cool breeze splashing across my face. While I was gazing out onto the water, I felt a chill run up my spine. I sat alone in this gorgeous setting, and many thoughts began filling my mind. I gazed back at our lot and tried to vision a new cabin being constructed on this site. I observed the oaks, maple, and birch trees that lined the shore. Then, I looked back at the sandy bare lot and trees located at the back end by the road.

"There is a great amount of work to be done before we can enjoy this place," I thought. "Trees need to be planted. Grass needs to grow, and a great deal of landscaping has to take place before this will ever begin to look respectable."

But then, I also realized the potential of this place and knew it was so much better than our lot across the road. I loved the spot, and I decided then I would do my part to make it beautiful. However, I also knew that I wasn't alone because my wife, brothers, and sisters-in-law shared my dream. I thanked God for the gift given to us poor insignificant Hall boys. I strolled back to our cabin and found Sandy already in bed. I snuggled in next to her and fell fast asleep.

OUR NEW CABIN

Before we could set up the final contract with Martin Homes, all of us had to meet at their showroom to pick out exactly what we wanted for our cabin. They had a standard line of products which were included in the price of the home. They also had more deluxe items if you wanted to upgrade and pay extra. We had to choose colors and styles of siding, shingles, cabinets, countertops, carpet, linoleum, light fixtures, faucets, door handles, and hardware. There were a lot of things we had to agree on, but it went smoothly. I don't recall any major disagreements.

It helped that we were all at the cabin the weekend before so Janet could explain what had to be done. We were able to talk about what we wanted. We also came to agreement on dividing the bedrooms, so each family could pick the color carpet they wanted for their room.

Our new cabin would have five bedrooms. Jon, Don, Steve, Marilyn, and I would each have our own bedroom for our families. Bob didn't need a bedroom because he lived in New York. He could use one of ours whenever he came to town.

"How do we decide who gets what bedrooms?" I asked as we all were sitting in the living room.

"Well, we will have two large bedrooms and three smaller rooms," stated Janet.

"Yes, and the three smaller bedrooms have a lake view," threw in Marilyn.

"We could draw straws to see who gets first choice," I proposed.

"I think that is too random," responded Sandy.

"How about the larger families get the larger bedrooms?" suggested Kathy.

"I think that is a good idea and a compromise," agreed Jon. "The smaller bedrooms have the lake view, and the larger bedrooms will accommodate the larger families."

"Jon, you have five children. Don, you have four. So, the larger bedrooms go to your two families," responded Steve.

"I'll take the end bedroom," stated Jon.

"That means you get two windows, and I only get one," responded Don.

"I'll flip you for it, little brother."

"No, that's okay. I like the middle bedroom."

"All right, two bedrooms are taken. How are we going to decide who gets the smaller ones?" questioned Steve.

"I'd like the end bedroom," said Marilyn.

Steve and I just gazed at each other.

"I'd like the one closest to the living room," Steve said after a while.

"Fine. I'll take the middle bedroom," I responded.

So, that's how we decided on the bedrooms.

"It will be so nice for each family to have their own bedroom. We can decorate them any way we want," laughed Janet.

"Each family will now have a place to stay and store their individual things." responded Sandy.

"We won't have to fight for space like we did in our smaller cabin," added Marilyn.

"What about the old cabin, Tommy?" questioned Steve.

"My friend, Larry, has already agreed to buy it. He agreed to give us $30,000 for the cabin. We need that money to pay for everything we have to hire out to get done. I'll contact Larry and swing the deal next week if it's all right with everyone," I stated.

Everyone nodded their heads in agreement.

"We'll need more than $30,000 before this deal is over," added Marilyn.

"I'll check on the loan with Martin Homes," responded Janet.

"What about our rooms when we are not up here?" questioned Jon.

"Good question," I said.

"As far as I'm concerned, anyone can use our room if we're not here," commented Janet.

"I think that's a good idea," I threw in.

"Yes, that would work as long as no one uses someone else's bedding, and they do not leave the room in a mess," agreed Sandy.

"Do you remember the guy that put the rock wall in our old cabin?" asked Steve.

"It was your friend, wasn't it?" responded Jon.

"Yes, and he's a great brick layer," added Steve.

"I think I know where you are going with this," Don said.

"We could use a nice fireplace at the end of the living room. I'll bet for a small fee and a case of beer, I could talk him into coming up here and building us a fireplace."

"That's a great idea, Steve," added Jon. "I really like the look of a used brick fireplace."

"Should I contact him?" asked Steve.

We all agreed.

"There is a great fireplace insert up by Leech Lake," added Don. "It has won an award for being a very efficient heater as well as a fireplace. It's called a Wilkening after its inventor. Should I check it out?"

"Absolutely," I said. "If it works out, I can get a trailer and haul it to the cabin."

So, we all had our little assignments and input into the completion of our new lake home. Some time later, I was sitting in my living room when the phone rang.

"Tom, answer the telephone!" Sandy yelled from the bathroom.

I ran to the phone, picked up the receiver, and said, "Hello?"

"Hello, Tom," Jon replied. "Janet made an appointment for all of us to meet Wednesday night at the office of Martin Homes in Edina. We'll be signing the contract for building our new cabin."

"Great, Jon! I'll call the others."

"We'll see you there at 7:30," responded Jon.

That Wednesday we all met in the lobby of Martin Homes' office. Marilyn, Jon and Janet, Don and Joy, Steve and Kathy, and Sandy and I were all there. Bill, who represented Martin Homes, met us in the lobby and invited us into his office. We all gathered around his desk as he pulled out our file. There were many papers for us to sign because we were taking out a mortgage with them for $39,324. Our payments would be $361 a month.

"Before we sign this agreement, let me go over a few items that need some explanation," Bill stated as he pulled out the floor plans for our new cabin. "First of all, you need a down payment of $4,152. We have agreed to build a five bedroom rambler with two bathrooms and a garage. We complete all the outside walls and work and frame in the inside walls. You complete the rest."

We all looked at each other with big smiles on our faces.

"We will be sending out two semi-trailers with all the material you will need to build this home," Bill went on. "That not only includes the lumber, but the windows, siding, roofing, carpet, flooring, fixtures, cupboards, and electrical and plumbing supplies as well. You need to be present when each truck arrives because it is your responsibility to unload it. We will send all the building material out on the first load. As soon as your building is standing and closed in, we will deliver all the sheet rock, wiring, plumbing, fixtures, cabinets, carpet and the rest of the finishing materials. Once again, you must be there to unload the trailer."

"That sounds great. As you can see, we will have enough bodies to unload the trailer," I responded with a grin on my face glancing around the room.

"Yes, I can see that," answered Bill observing us strong healthy looking Hall boys.

"Just let us know when the truck will arrive at our property, and we'll be there," stated Jon.

We signed the papers and wrote Martin Homes a check for $4,152. Bill shook each of our hands.

"This is a pretty amazing transaction. I have never seen anything quite like it. I hope you enjoy your new lake home, and I want to wish you all the best of luck."

We all stood around in the parking lot talking before driving home. Excitement was seen on all our faces

"Now, the work begins. Martin Homes will hire a carpenter from the area to construct our cabin and garage. They will send him out to talk to us," stated Janet. "He will do as much of the inside work as we want him to do, and we'll do the rest."

At the end of July, Larry Martin had purchased our old cabin for $30,000. That money was used for our down payment and the rest for all the other work needed to complete the new cabin. Larry let us stay in our old cabin until our new cabin was constructed. He was willing to wait so I could be up there to work with the carpenters and see that everything was going all right, and we'd have a place to keep our stuff.

"Well, we're on our way!" stated Jon as we departed to our separate automobiles.

That night, Sandy and I were sitting on the couch discussing our cabin project after putting the kids to bed.

"Do you realize what you got us into?" stated Sandy gazing deeply into my eyes.

"Not really. I think we'll just have to take things as they come."

"We are building a five bedroom home, Tommy, not just a little cabin."

"Yes, I know that, but it's not like I'm doing all the work. I have four brothers to help me," I responded.

"Yes, you do, but Dave is not here. You'll have to take the leadership. Are you ready for that?"

"I think so," I replied with not much confidence.

"Tommy, the carpenter will build the structure, but what about all the rest of the work?"

"What do you mean?"

"Who will do the foundation, the electrical work, the plumbing, and put in the pump?"

"I don't know. I hadn't thought about all that."

"I think you need to talk to Roy. He built his home in Golden Valley," she suggested.

Roy was married to Sandy's sister, Shirley, and had helped us frame up our first cabin. He was very knowledgeable in this area. So, I called Roy and talked with him for hours. He told me that I needed to get a hold of subcontractors to do all the jobs that the carpenter would not do.

First, I had to contact a cement layer to lay out the foundation according to the floor plans. I talked to some local people who recommended a cement man from Siren. He agreed to lay the foundation on a weekend. I called Roy and asked him to be with me when the foundation was laid. He agreed.

I was up at the cabin with my family as well as Roy and Shirley when the cement man arrived. He drove into our driveway in his pickup truck. I greeted him and offered him a cup of coffee.

"My name is Tom," I said as we walked into our cabin. I introduced him to Sandy, Roy, and Shirley.

"I'm Richard Shutt," he stated.

Richard was a big burly man in his early thirties. He asked to look at the plans.

"This shouldn't be too bad," he said. "I have the blocks coming shortly and the cement truck coming tomorrow to lay the slab for your garage."

His crew of three men arrived, as did a load of blocks for the foundation. The blocks were unloaded, and the men went to work. They measured out the dimensions, staked out the area, and began laying the blocks. I was amazed at the size of the cabin, which seemed to stretch the entire width of our lot. After the first layer was completed, Richard took a tape measure and measured diagonally. A huge smile came across his face, and he called me over.

"Look at this, Tom!" he said. "It is less than a quarter of an inch off. That is about as square as I can make it."

"That's cool!" I responded.

When Richard finished the foundation, he looked at the plans. He called me over and told me that we didn't need as many pilings down the center of our cabin as the plans called for. I asked Roy to look at the plans, and he did so.

"I think you better follow the plans and include all the pilings to have good solid support," Roy stated confidently.

"Will do!" responded Richard.

When the foundation was completed, Richard staked out the area for our garage. After he had completed it, he and his crew left. They would return the next day to lay the slab. I thanked him for his good work.

After he left, Roy and I took a closer look at the foundation.

"Richard is good at what he does," Roy said. "He did a nice job on this foundation. However, it was good that we were here and that he complied with the plans for all the pilings in the center of the building."

"I'm glad you were here, Roy. I didn't know what to tell him."

Just then, Roy glanced at the staking for the garage and then back at the cabin.

"Tom, the garage doesn't look square to the cabin. It looks a little off."

"Really, Roy? I don't see it."

Roy was a surveyor and landscape architect, and he had a good eye. He checked it out and sure enough, it wasn't square. The next day, we had Richard square it up. He seemed to appreciate and respect Roy's knowledge.

When Richard and his crew completed their work, the foundation and garage were ready for the carpenter to begin his work. I learned that I needed to be resourceful, ask questions, and be there when the subcontractors were working. The process was in motion, and I needed help, support, and prayer to make all this happen. The leadership would be a real challenge for me.

After the foundation was laid, I realized we needed to drill a well for our water. I contacted Pete Moser who had done some work for us on our other lot. He lived in a small house behind a little grocery store on County Road A.

I strolled into his store and asked for Pete. The lady behind the counter dialed a number. About five minutes later, Pete emerged from the back of the store.

"Hey, Tom, what can I do for you?"

"I need a well dug. Do you want the job?"

"Yes! I can dig it for you next week."

"We own the lot right next to Vandergon's," I said. "The foundation is laid, and we need a well before the carpenters begin construction."

"We'll need to go down over one hundred feet. There is a good water vane there. Will next Wednesday work for you?"

"Yes, I will be there with a thermos of coffee and some rolls for our break."

"Thanks, Tom," Pete replied. "I'll be there with my son, Jim. We'll find some good water for you."

The next Wednesday, Pete and Jim showed up with their truck and all the drilling equipment.

"Where do you want your well, Tom?" asked Pete.

"Right inside our foundation, Pete," I responded.

Pete and Jim set up their equipment, fitted a sand point on three inch steel tubing, and began sinking the pipes. When they were about 110 feet down, water began bubbling and coming up the pipe. Pete jumped back.

"Tom, I think we hit an artesian well," he said excitedly. "The water is coming up the pipe without a pump,"

He expected the water to come flowing out of the top of the pipe. However, the water stopped about three feet from the top.

"I've never seen anything like this, Tom. I thought we hit an artesian well, but it stopped just short of the top. All you need is a shallow well pump, and you will have good pressure and great water!"

He installed a pump and turned it on. Water came shooting out of the top.

"Get me a glass, and let's have a taste," suggested Pete.

I gave him a glass, and he filled it with water. It was crystal clear. He tasted it and gave it to me. I tasted it, and it was good.

"What do you think, Tom?" questioned Pete.

"It's not bad, Pete, but I can taste pipe dope."

"That's because I needed to use pipe dope to connect the sections as we were drilling. That taste will soon disappear."

Sure enough, the taste went away, and we have great water. We have never had rust or a brown color in our toilets. Thanks to Pete Moser, we are blessed with great water. We brought a sample of water home and had it tested at the University of Minnesota. The result was great pure water.

About the third weekend in August, we were all up at our old cabin having breakfast. Martin Homes had decided to send up the first loaded semi that weekend. We needed to be there to unload the trailer. My friend and colleague, Jim Sorteberg, was with us to help unload the trailer. Jim was big and strong and a very good friend.

"How is that semi going to back into our lot?" questioned Jon.

"Yeah, I wondered about that too," stated Don. "Our road is very narrow."

"I've already talked to Harold, our neighbor. He's agreed to let the truck pull into his driveway and back into our lot."

"You've thought of everything, Tommy," shouted Steve.

"Yes, but I had a little help from Sandy," I responded.

Just then, Jon got up from the table.

"I hear the roar of a huge semi. I think our truck has arrived."

We all jumped up from the table and rushed out the door. I was leading the pack. When I arrived at the top of our hill, I was amazed at the size of the semi on our little private road. It was parked in front of our lot and the driver was standing outside looking at our empty lot. I ran down to greet him.

"Hi, I'm Tom Hall. I guess you found us all right. Did you have any trouble finding us?"

"My name is John. I just had a little trouble crossing the narrow bridge on the St. Croix River coming into Wisconsin."

"Do you think you can back it in so we can unload?"

"I'll need to drive up on some of your neighbor's property to make the swing."

"You can drive up on Harold's property," I stated pointing up the road and diagonally.

"That will work!" responded John as he hopped into his cab. He took two or three swings but eventually managed to back into the middle of our empty lot. He jumped out of the cab, cracked the seal, and swung open the huge doors to reveal a full load of building material.

"It's all yours, guys," he said. "You have your work cut out for you!"

The forty-foot trailer was totally loaded from front to back with building materials.

"All this material needs to be taken out and organized into some meaningful order. We should put the material that is similar into piles around the lot so the carpenters can easily find things," I stated.

It took the five of us about four hours of sweat labor to unload the semi. I was grateful Jim Sorteberg had agreed to help us. We sorted out the material as best we could to make things easier for the carpenters. With all the material out of the truck and on the ground, it was quite a scene seeing everything lying in piles. When we finally got to the end of the forty foot trailer, Jim grabbed the last piece of lumber. He walked out of the trailer with a huge smile on his face.

"This is the piece of lumber we've been looking for," he stated. "If we would have begun with this piece of wood, we would have saved ourselves a lot of work."

My brothers and I just looked at each other and burst into laughter as we realized he was messing with our minds.

I tried to visualize it all being put together, but just couldn't quite seem to get a picture in my mind. After a very exhausting day, we ambled back to our cabin for some much needed rest. Jim and I were sitting with a cup of coffee on the flat roof of our boathouse overlooking the back bay and the wilderness beyond.

"Thanks for your help, Jim!"

"No problem, Tom. I enjoyed helping and getting to know your brothers. They're quite an interesting group of guys. It's quite a project that you have going here!"

"Yes, and it looks like the leadership falls on my shoulders. I don't know if I'm up for the challenge."

"You're the leader. There's no question about that."

"How do you know that, Jim?"

"It's very obvious when you observe what is happening. You're too close to the situation, so you probably don't even notice. Your brothers look to you for everything, and work doesn't get done until you initiate."

"Wow, thanks for that explanation! To me, we are all adults and in this together."

'You're right, Tom, but you need a leader in this undertaking. Since they all look to you anyway, why fight it? Just take the mantle, delegate responsibility, and make it happen for your family. You don't need to worry. You have all the resources you need with your brothers and Sandy's support. I'm excited to see how this all plays out for you," Jim encouraged.

"You know, Jim, this was all my big brother's idea. Did you ever meet Dave? He taught in our school district at Irondale High School."

"As a matter-of-fact, I did. I was on a committee with him. He was a good leader and a great guy."

"He was our leader throughout this cabin project! He told me it was a lot of work. He said

I would have to step up and build a home on our other lot."

"Well, Tom, he was right. I have no doubt that you will step up and lead. I would follow you anywhere, and so will your brothers."

"Thanks for the encouragement, Jim," I said gratefully.

The next day, we were all moaning with aches, pains, and sore muscles. Everyone left that Sunday evening leaving Sandy and me with our children to meet our carpenter the next day. On Monday, a car drove into our driveway. An older man in his fifties got our of his car and knocked on our door.

"Hi, my name is Clarence Wilde," he said. "I've been hired by Martin Homes to build your cabin."

"I'm Tom, and this is my wife, Sandy," I said. "My brothers and I own the property and are building this cabin together. The property is across the road on the big side of the lake. The foundation has been laid, and the slab for the garage has been poured. We emptied a trailer of supplies this weekend and tried to sort out the materials as best we could. I'll walk over to our lot with you."

We cut across our backyard, headed down the private dirt road, and turned into our lot. It looked pretty bare and sandy except for the piles of building material all over the lot. The foundation and slab also stood out. Clarence looked over the material with a puzzled expression on his face. He didn't say anything for quite a while. Finally, he spoke up, and I didn't like what I heard.

"This isn't the small cabin I was expecting to see. You have a large five bedroom home here with an unattached garage. I'm sorry, but I can't take this project. I have many people in front of you that have work for me to do. I didn't realize this was such a huge project. No, I can't do it!"

"You agreed to do this work, and now you don't want the job?"

"You're looking at a two month project. I'm sorry, but you'll have to find someone else."

"Are you sure you don't want to build this home for us?"

"Yes, I'm sure!" he said emphatically.

We walked back to our cabin in silence.

"It was nice meeting you, Clarence," I said as he headed for his car.

"Yes, it was nice meeting you too, Tom. I'm sorry that I can't help you out."

I walked into our cabin with my head down.

"What's the matter, Hon?" Sandy asked.

"The carpenter said the job was too big and he has too many people ahead of us, so he won't take the job," I responded.

"What do we do now?"

"The only thing I can think to do is pray," I responded.

So, that's what I did.

"Dear Father," I prayed. "We need a carpenter to build our cabin. Martin Homes hired this guy,

Clarence. He doesn't want this big of a project. He said we were way down on the list. I don't know what to do. Please help us find a good carpenter. Everything is here and ready to go. I need an answer because I don't know what to do. Thank you for hearing my prayer. In Jesus' name, amen!"

That night, I went to bed very dejected and tired. I must have been very tired because I can't remember hitting the pillow. In the morning some noise startled me. I listened intently! It sounded like the pounding of hammers. I walked into the kitchen in my underwear.

"Do you hear that pounding?"

"Yes, and it sounds like it's coming from our lot," Sandy replied. "You'd better go check it out."

I quickly got dressed, scampered out the door, and headed for our lot as the hammer pounding got louder. When I got to our lot, I noticed Clarence and three young men working on our cabin. I couldn't believe my eyes! Clarence had just told me that he wouldn't do this project. Now, the next morning, I was observing him and his young crew constructing our cabin.

"Tom, it's a good morning, isn't it?" he asked as I moved toward him.

"I thought you wouldn't take this job," I said. "You said it was too big for you."

"It's not too big for me. I just had other priorities."

"What changed your mind?"

"These three boys are my sons. They are all excellent carpenters. We have never built a home together. This is a perfect opportunity for us to build a home from scratch. It will be a good learning experience for my sons, and we'll build you a great home."

"I believe you will, Clarence. Thank you. I wasn't sure where I would find a carpenter."

"Well, now you have four of us!"

I strolled back to my cabin in disbelief

"Is that how you answer my prayers, Father? Thank you, and please bless their hands as they build this home for us. Please make it a good experience for us as well as for them," I prayed.

"Sandy, we have our builder," I said as I opened the door. "Clarence has three sons, and they are going to build a beautiful cabin for the Hall family. I can't believe it!"

"What did he say, Tommy?"

"He changed his mind and thought it would be a good project for him and his sons. I thanked him, and he went back to work."

"Well, all I can say is this will be an interesting journey, Tom."

It was exciting to watch as our new cabin began to take shape and form. Two of Clarence's sons worked on the garage while Clarence and his oldest son began constructing the cabin. The garage went up fairly quickly and was completed. It looked great. The crew of four then worked together to tackle the home. It was framed up fairly quickly.

As I watched this family working together, I soon realized they were a competent crew. Each one had a responsibility. When the sons had questions, they would ask their father who quickly supplied the answers. It was a great setting for this family, and they loved working together. Their own home was about fifteen minutes away, so Clarence's wife and daughter would come over with lunch for the four hungry workers. It was truly a family project. This seemed very fitting because our building was being built for multiple families. In a sense, two families were working together for the same end.

One weekend, Steve and I were at the new cabin examining the carpenter's work. We noticed how small the front window in the living room was which we thought would capture a great view of the lake.

"Clarence, can't you give us a bigger window to capture this great view of our gorgeous lake?" questioned Steve.

"Would it be possible to put in a sliding glass door?" I threw in.

Clarence looked at the window he just put in and thought intently.

"I wouldn't recommend a glass door if you have children running in and out all the time," he said. "I can get a window unit which includes a large picture window and two adjacent windows on each end. I think it would capture the view you are looking for."

Steve looked at me.

"That would be great, Clarence!" I said. "Let's make that happen!"

The next week when Sandy and I walked into the cabin, we saw the new window unit had been installed. It revealed a beautiful wide panoramic view of our lake.

"We will enjoy this view for years to come!" I exclaimed giving Sandy a hug.

Clarence and his sons worked steadily for over a month. They put up the walls, nailed the ceiling joists in place, installed plywood sheathing and shingles on the roof, put on the front and back decks, hung all the windows and exterior doors, and put on the siding and exterior trim. Inside, they put particle board on the floor and framed in all the rooms. It was now closed in and ready for the second semi to bring all the interior finishing materials. That included sheetrock and taping, wiring and plumbing supplies, sinks, toilets, showers, interior doors and hardware, light fixtures, cabinets and countertops, all the woodwork, trim and baseboards, carpet for five bedrooms and living room and hallway, linoleum for the kitchen, dining area, and both bathrooms, a water heater, and electric baseboard heaters for all the rooms.

Martin Homes had paid Clarence to put up the base structure. It was now our responsibility to complete the inside with all the new stuff delivered. At this point, I think it was our wives who figured out there was no way us brothers could complete the inside. It would take us a couple years and then probably not be done right. We decided to contact Clarence to see if he would be interested in doing some work on the inside. It was getting late in the fall, so we hoped he would work with his sons over the winter. Because he lived so close, Clarence again thought this would be a good learning experience for his boys. He said he wouldn't do any of the plumbing or electrical work. We would have to hire someone to do that. We told him we could do all the painting and staining and lay all the carpets and linoleum. We needed him to do the sheetrock and ceilings, hang all the interior doors and kitchen cabinets, and do the woodwork trim and baseboards. He said he would work with our electrician and plumber on the timing of different things. Our wives were really happy everything would get done right in this cabin.

Before Clarence closed in the walls, I contacted an electrician and plumber. I asked some questions from merchants I had gotten to know in Webster and received two names that I contacted. The electrician, Morris Irwin, came out and quoted us a price. I hired him. He and his wife worked together and did an outstanding job wiring our cabin.

Nels Koerper was the plumber we hired. He lived just south of Webster. He connected all the sinks, toilets, water heater, outside spigots, and set up for a washing machine. He loved doing new construction and did a great job with the plumbing. Nels and I became good friends.

"Tom, I've finished the plumbing," he stated as we looked at his work. "I angled the copper tubing so that you won't have to blow out the lines when you close up this place for winter. I've used the principle of gravity to make sure when you drain the lines, the water will flow downward and drain completely. If you have any problems, just give me a call. I'll be your plumber in residence and will keep you happy with that area of your home."

"Thanks for your good work, Nels," I responded and handed him a check with a smile on my face.

Both Nels and the electrician did some of their work in the fall and completed the rest in the spring after Clarence was done. That fall, before the walls were closed in, we also installed our fireplace. Steve contacted his friend, Dave Christy, and he agreed to build us a fireplace. Don and I drove up to Leech Lake, picked up the fireplace insert, and brought it to the cabin. The following week in early October, Steve's friend built a beautiful used brick fireplace around the insert. It worked great and was very efficient.

It was getting late in the fall and beginning to get cold. Clarence and his sons could use the fireplace to keep warm as they worked over the winter. We already had our well dug underneath our cabin but had not hooked up our septic system. Pete Moser would have to come back in the spring and hook everything up, so we had no water yet. We needed to put in a Mound system because our water table was so high. We had contacted a local company who would install it in the spring. We did have electricity though.

By early March in the spring of 1980, the carpenters' part of our project was pretty much completed.

Everything was done except for some of the interior trim to be put on after we put up paneling. We settled up with Clarence and left a small amount to be paid when that trim was completed. Clarence and his sons had done excellent work.

FINISHING UP

One weekend in early March, Jon, Don, Steve, and I drove up to the cabin to put a primer coat of paint on all the walls with the exception of our bedrooms. It was our first trip after the carpenters completed their work. When we arrived, we were all amazed at what had already been accomplished and were realizing what the future had in store for us.

As we were painting, we got in a silly mood and were laughing and joking with each other. Jon had brought up some wine, and Don had consumed a little too much. During our break, Don had us on the floor with one liners that wouldn't quit.

As we neared the end of our project on Sunday night, my responsibility was to finish priming the small back bathroom. It was a closed in space with the door shut, and the fumes from the primer began affecting my performance. However, I was bound and determined to complete the job. I was painting the final corner of the ceiling when the fumes hit me like a ton of bricks. I fell off the ladder and stumbled into the living room where my brothers were painting. They gazed at me stumbling into the living room, slurring my words, and not making any sense. Finally, Jon took me out on the deck to get some fresh air. I breathed in the fresh air and regained my composure. I walked back into the living room. My brothers were on the floor laughing uncontrollably.

"I've never seen Tom in a situation like that," Jon laughed.

"Yeah, his eyes were rolling, and he didn't make any sense. I wish I had that on film. You were a sight for sore eyes, Tom. It was like you were stone drunk and wanted us to understand what you were saying," laughed Don.

"I know you hadn't been drinking any wine, Tommy, but you weren't making any sense," chuckled Steve.

"I know it was funny, but those fumes really got to me," I said. "I just have a little corner left, but I don't want to go back in there. It was kind of scary."

"You don't have to go back in there, Tom. I'll finish the bathroom," stated Jon. "Maybe it was more serious than we thought, but I have never seen you in such a compromised position. It was hilarious!"

As we brothers drove home that weekend, we realized something special was happening between us. We had gone through so much adversity growing up in near poverty. We had suffered the deaths of our father and brother. We were all married now and beginning our careers and families. We were working on a special and beautiful place that would hold our extended family together for years to come. Sibling rivalry had run its course. We were grown up and investing our resources in a place for ourselves and our expanding families.

The following weekend, my brothers and I headed back to our lake place to begin staining all the woodwork. I drove and Jon, Don, and Steve rode with me. We were driving up Highway 35 after stopping at McDonalds for coffee.

"What do we have left to do before we can begin enjoying our new place?" Jon asked as he took a sip from his coffee cup.

Jon was the mechanical one in the family and a real leader. He was also the wildest of all of us. He always moved close to the line to see just how far he could go. Sometimes, he even crossed the line and usually got into trouble.

"We have a lot of projects to complete before we can really enjoy this place," I commented with my eyes on the road.

"What still needs to be done?" prompted Don.

Don had endured a very tough winter. His wife had left him in the fall and moved to Minot, North Dakota to be close to her parents. She took their four children with her. Don had gone through a rough divorce and was struggling personally. Despite all of this, he was still our hardest working brother. If

Don had a project to do, he wouldn't quit until it was completed. Don and Steve were close friends.

"I'll have to contact Hopkins Landscaping about installing our Mound system."

"What's a Mound system?" questioned Steve.

Steve was my youngest brother. He was a hockey player and had completed a great career at the University of Minnesota on a full athletic scholarship. During his junior year, his team finished second in the nation. Steve got a degree in psychology, but he could not find a job in his field. After spending time working as a journeyman painter, he had started a new company selling and servicing fire extinguishers. Steve was also a hard worker. We would need his painting skills often.

"Where have you been?" laughed Jon. "We've only been talking about a Mound system for about a year."

"Shut up, Jon! Explain a Mound system again to me, Tommy."

"We can't put in a septic tank on our lot because the water table is too high," I said. "We did a perc test last year, and they found water at ten feet. So, we need another way to dispose of our water and waste. I contacted a man at Hopkins Landscaping who recommended a Mound system. They will install two holding tanks. When we flush the toilets or drain the water, the water will flow into the first tank. Then, it will be pumped into the second tank. From the second tank, water will be pumped into the mound and then dispersed into the soil through plastic lines with holes in them. They have to bring in equipment to bury the tanks and build up a mound. It will be quite a project!"

"So, do we have to be careful not to flush too often or drain water very carefully?" asked Steve.

"Not really. It is a very efficient way to remove dirty water and waste. We shouldn't have to clean out our tanks very often, but we'll just have to see how it works," commented Jon.

"It won't be cheap either!" I explained. "However, we'll only have a holding tank until we receive approval on the Mound."

"How much will it cost us?" questioned Donny.

"About five thousand dollars," I stated.

"Yikes! Do we have that kind of money?" responded Steve.

"We got $30,000 for our old cabin and have been using that to pay for all the work we've been doing so far. We should have enough money. However, I think we'll use up all of that money before we are done with everything," I added.

"How much will we need to pay each month?" questioned Jon.

"It's a good thing our lot is paid for. I think we'll each have to put in about $100 every month. Sandy will figure that out for us."

"What else needs to be accomplished?" asked Jon.

"We need to paint the outside of the cabin and the garage. We already bought a dark brown stain. Steve, you can take the leadership on that project.

We need to paint some walls inside also and install paneling. We can all do that. The linoleum and carpets have to be laid but not until all painting, staining, and wallpapering is done. Jon, you will take leadership on that. We also have to clear the land and plant some grass seed. Finally, each of us is responsible to complete with paint or wallpaper our individual bedrooms. It sounds like a lot of work, but there are four of us. The girls will help with our individual rooms. I think we should have it all done by the end of June."

It was amazing how it all came together. Hopkins came out in April with their huge equipment and put in a large holding tank we used until our Mound system was approved. It was not until the end of September that our Mound system was finally completed. We were really happy to get it because we had to clean out the holding tank several times that summer. After Nels and Pete Moser completed their work in April, our water system worked perfectly. Jon and I stained our front and back deck.

Steve headed up our painting. We used brushes and rollers to complete the outside staining of our cabin and garage. Our carpenter had installed metal eaves, so we didn't need to paint them. I really appreciated this. I hated painting eaves because the paint would always drip on my face.

The women really got involved in the decorating project. We put up oak paneling in the living room on one interior wall and the walls on each side of the fireplace. On the wall opposite the fireplace that goes from the front door through the kitchen to the back door, we paneled a third of the way up from the floor, and painted the rest. We paneled a third of the way up in the dining room as well. We also wall-papered both bathrooms, the kitchen, dining area, and the long hallway.

The interesting part of these projects came when each family decorated their own bedrooms. Steve and Kathy wallpapered their room. You don't ever want to wallpaper your room with your wife. I watched with much amusement as they struggled with this project and with each other. It wasn't a pretty scene. I learned by watching them because Sandy and I also decided to wallpaper our bedroom as well. To avoid any arguments, I decided to keep my mouth shut and do whatever she said. It was difficult. I was ordered around a lot, but the project was completed without any problems. Jon and Janet wallpapered their room and struggled as much as Steve and Kathy. Don painted and paneled his room, and Marilyn and her son, Doug, painted their room. Everything turned out well.

After all the messy projects of painting, staining, and wallpapering were done, Jon instructed us in laying the linoleum and carpets. We had already picked them out, and they had been delivered in our second semi from Martin Homes. This completed the kitchen, dining room, bathrooms, and living areas.

The inside of the cabin was pretty much done. We had contacted Clarence after our paneling was up to complete the finishing trim but hadn't seen him. We discovered that the final trim projects were not his priority. I realized we would have to complete the final trim ourselves.

I contacted Roy again and asked him for some help. He and his wife drove up one weekend, and Roy installed all the finishing trim on the paneling for us while I helped as his gopher. We also attached legs to our big kitchen table to make it more sturdy. It had just been sitting on a barrel.

"Thanks for the help, Roy," I said. "Now, it looks finished."

"No problem, Tom. I enjoyed helping you out with this project. Your family is really going to enjoy this place in the future. It is a great cabin on a gorgeous lake and has an unbelievable setting."

Outside there was much work to be done also. We got out our riding lawn mower and hooked up an old box spring tied to a rope. After we cleared off all the vegetation from our lawn, we dragged the box spring round and round until the yard was smooth like a baseball diamond. Then, we spread grass seed and raked it into the soil. We watered it frequently, and soon a nice lawn appeared.

On each side of our lot, our neighbors had planted small Norway and white Pine trees to define their property lines. We had large birch, maple, and oak trees in the front by the lake and way in the back of our lot by the road. Otherwise, the rest of our lot was fairly bare. I bought three ash trees at a Holiday Store for a dollar and planted them in the front and backyard. My neighbor, Don Vandergon, told me

I would die before they grew up because they had no branches and only came up to my waist. He was wrong!

Let me describe our cabin. Our cabin is a long rambler with a crawl space underneath it. It is built on cement blocks that are three to four rows high. We stained the wood siding a dark brown color.

When you enter our cabin from the back door, which faces the road, there is a bathroom on the right and the kitchen on the left. The kitchen is long and narrow. It has a sink in a long countertop on one side with a window above it facing the backyard. There are cupboards above on both sides and all along underneath. Each family has their own cupboard in the kitchen. The refrigerator and stove are on the other side with cupboards above and on each side of the stove. The kitchen opens to our dining area where we placed the large table Dave had built in his woodworking shop at school. It could seat about ten to twelve people. As you face the table from the kitchen, a large double window on the left looks out to the backyard. Straight ahead is a large single window that looks out to the side of the cabin. On the right side of the dining room, a large archway opens to the living room and a magnificent view of the lake through our picture window. You can see this lake view sitting at our big table, and you feel like you're sitting on top of the water because that's all you see. It's amazing.

The living room has a used brick fireplace on one end and the large picture window in the front capturing our view of the lake. The oak paneled wall separates the living room from the kitchen. The front door is next to the picture window and leads to our large, rectangular deck. The deck turned out to be a great area for grilling, eating, and watching the kids play in the lake.

A long hallway stretches from the end of the living room down to all our bedrooms. On the right hand side of the hallway, there are four doors. The first goes to a hall closet where we store games and toys. Next to the closet is our main bathroom. Don's bedroom is next, and Jon's bedroom is last at the end of the hallway. On the left hand side of the hallway are three doors. The first leads to Steve's room, the second leads to mine, and Marilyn's bedroom is at the end. Each room in the cabin has an electric baseboard heater. Our fireplace can also heat up the cabin very efficiently.

The wide steps on the front deck descend to a narrow front lawn. The huge sandy beach is in front of the lawn and descends down to our beautiful spring fed lake. The water is rather shallow at first, making a great swim area for little children. We have a huge lawn in the backyard that stretches from the cabin towards the garage, the driveway, and Peninsula Road.

For a long time it seemed like every weekend was a "work" weekend. Through all the hard work, we finally completed all our projects. With four of us working pretty hard, it didn't really seem that difficult. That's because we always took time off to play too. We spent much time swimming, fishing, and water skiing behind our new to us aluminum boat that was powered by a 60 horse Johnson.

Leonard Cison was my neighbor back in Minneapolis. He helped me with many cabin projects. He built us a roll-out dock with a bench at the end. This new dock suited our needs. He also built us a really heavy iron boat lift. He brought it up in pieces and welded it together at the cabin. Leonard also built us a basketball backboard which we installed over our garage door. When we needed a new boat, Leonard and I found a used boat with a hole in the front. We bought it for four hundred dollars and spent a weekend patching it up with fiberglass. To power the boat, we found a used 90 horsepower outboard motor. It was a perfect ski boat for our family because it had enough power for our needs. This boat pulled our children all over the lake for hours on water skis, knee boards, and tubes.

Another friend of mine came to the cabin and put in our blacktop driveway. He brought his Bobcat and filled in a large depression in the back of the lot. He also dug a hole by the door leading to our pump under the cabin. We installed treated lumber around it. With the driveway complete and the basketball hoop up, we had a great place to play basketball on the smooth flat surface.

We bought a Sunfish sailboat and a Grumman canoe from Trout Lake Camp. The camp turns their boats over each year. Since I had worked there for two summers, they sold them to me at a very reasonable price. We also purchased a small fishing boat from my neighbor, Leonard, and Steve got a 7 horse Johnson fishing motor for it. Jon and Steve also made a horseshoe pit for us to use in the backyard.

Over time, we made various other improvements to our cabin. However, the stage was now set for us to come and play. And play we did!

CABIN LIFE

With our new cabin now completed, it was quite different coming to the lake. Each family had their own bedroom, so we no longer had to figure out sleeping arrangements for all who came. We often had slept two families together in the small back bedroom at our old cabin. That was very interesting with small children. Now, we could leave our beds made and ready for us when we came again. We no longer had to haul all our sleeping bags, pillows, and bedding back and forth each week. That really lightened our load. If anyone used our room, they would always use their own bedding or sleeping bags on top of ours. Sandy and I had a double bed in our room. We also had a bunk bed for Mike and Katie we had gotten from Trout Lake Camp. Each family had enough beds in their bedroom to accommodate their family.

Each family also had their own cupboard in the kitchen. We all had a place to put the food we brought and could leave food and not have to tote things back and forth. Each family also got one shelf and a drawer or the extra shelf in the refrigerator to keep their cold food. Our wives say it's amazing how much you can squeeze on one shelf. We all respected each other's territory and did not take food from others' cupboards or fridge shelves. Because everyone could come at the same time now, we never knew how many would be there. We stopped trying to plan meals together. Instead, each family planned their own meals and snacks and only brought what they would need.

So, each family was set up with its own bedroom and kitchen storage area. The rest of the kitchen, dining room, living room, and bathrooms belong to all of us. The only brother who didn't have a bedroom was Bob. This was because he lived in New York and only came to the cabin for one week during the summer. When his family came, there was always at least one room available for him.

We had a wonderful summer together during our first year. Many of our children were elementary school age. Mike and Katie were ten and eight years old. All the cousins really enjoyed being together at the cabin.

It was so different being on the big side of the lake. Our old cabin was on the back bay, which was covered with weeds and lily pads. The view was gorgeous, but we couldn't spend much time in the water. On this side of the peninsula, we had a beautiful swimming beach as well as a great view. The water is shallow near the beach but gradually gets deeper. At about thirty yards out, the water is up to your neck.

North Sand Lake is about a half mile across and about two miles long. It covers about a thousand acres including the back bay. The lake is spring fed and crystal clear. When you peer down, you can see your toes clearly. When you dive underwater, it's so clear that you don't even need a mask to see.

All the brothers and Marilyn came up to the cabin almost every weekend during the summer. There was room for all of us. Our families played hard all weekend. We usually waited until Sunday to cut the lawn and complete any other projects needing to get done.

My room was on the lake side. I remember one particular morning. We'd had the new cabin for a couple summers. I rolled over in bed and peered out the window. The sun was coming up in the east giving off rays of orange and pink. It was breathtaking!

"Sandy, wake up and take a gander out of our window."

"Go back to sleep, Tommy. It's too early to get up!"

"No! You've got to see this!" I answered shaking her shoulders.

She rolled over and joined me at the window.

"Wow! That is spectacular!" she whispered with eyes as big as saucers.

The kids were still sound asleep.

"I don't think I'll ever get used to this, Sandy."

"Tommy, it's beautiful! It is almost surreal. It's nature at its best announcing a new day," she said softly.

"Let's get dressed, make some coffee, and sit on the deck to enjoy the show before everyone gets up," I suggested.

"That sounds like a plan," responded Sandy.

We quietly got dressed and used the bathroom. Sandy headed for the kitchen to put on a pot of coffee. I walked out the front door and sat on the deck facing the lake. It was a clear day in June. The sun brightened things up considerably as it rose higher in the sky.

"Open the door, Tom," Sandy whispered from the door.

I jumped up, opened the door, took the tray of coffee and donuts from her hands, and set it on the table. Sandy sat down, and I brought her coffee and a donut. I went back to fetch mine and sat beside her. I felt a cool breeze splash against my face as I placed both hands around my coffee cup. The waves were gently splashing against the shore, and white billowy clouds were scattered against the azure sky. I put my feet up on a chair, sipped my coffee, and inhaled the fresh oxygen that filled the air.

"It is so quiet and peaceful up here, Tommy," Sandy commented.

"Enjoy it while you can. Soon, everyone will be up, and we'll both wonder where the quiet went."

Sandy and I sat quietly enjoying our coffee and the peaceful environment. Soon, things began stirring in the cabin behind us. Everyone began waking up. Janet and Jon came out with cups of coffee to join us.

"How long have you guys been out here?" questioned Jon pulling up a chair beside me.

"Long enough to observe the most spectacular sunrise I've ever seen, little brother," I stated as I finished my last sip of coffee.

"The pinks, oranges, and purples were magnificent," responded Sandy as Janet sat down in a chair next to her husband.

"When should we put the caramel rolls in the oven, Sandy?" asked Janet.

"Let's wait about fifteen minutes, so everyone is up. I'm also making scrambled eggs for everyone this morning."

Caramel rolls were a tradition of ours and had been for years. The girls always made them the night before. In the morning, after the dough had risen, the rolls were placed in the oven. They came out fresh and gooey with caramel spread all over them.

Sandy and Janet finished their coffee and went into the kitchen. Jon and I remained on the deck.

"What do we have going today, Tommy?"

"I don't know, Jon. Do you have anything in mind?"

"I thought maybe you could help Chris get up on skis."

"I was talking to Mike last night around the campfire. He said he could get Chris up," I said.

"How could he do that?" Jon inquired.

"Mike said he would ski with slalom skis. Chris would put his feet in the cups behind Mike's and put his arms around Mike's waist. Then, when the boat pulls Mike up, Chris would get up behind him. That would give Chris the feel of what it is like on top of the water."

"Do you think it will work?" questioned Jon.

"I think it might. We'll have to try it after breakfast."

After enjoying a delicious breakfast of scrambled eggs and caramel rolls, I walked down to the dock and lowered our speedboat. I backed it out of the shore station and cruised around the lake to warm up the motor. When I came back, everyone was on the dock ready to do some serious water skiing.

"I'll go first, Tom," yelled Jim, Marilyn's youngest son.

Jim loved to ski and could go forever. He was already in the water with his life jacket on.

"Jon, jump in the boat and spot for Jim," I yelled pulling the boat next to the dock.

Jon came running out on the dock and climbed into the boat.

"Are you going to try to get Chris up by holding on to Mike?" questioned Jon as we circled the boat into position.

"Yeah! Right after I pull Jim, we'll try to get Chris up on skis hanging on to Mike."

Jon whirled the ski rope around his head and propelled it almost on Jim's lap.

"Nice shot, Uncle Jon," yelled Jim as he raised the tips of his skis just above the water.

I slowly moved the boat forward to take up the slack in the rope.

"Hit it!" Jim yelled.

I pushed the throttle forward. Jim popped out of the water like a cork and swung immediately outside the wake. I took him for a long ride and swung by our cabin thinking he would let go of the rope. Instead, he dropped one ski and wanted more. We took him around the point where the water was smooth and quiet. He looked great as he cut in and out of the wake. Finally, he pointed his thumb over his right shoulder indicating he wanted to be brought in. I circled the boat and headed back to our cabin. As I cruised by the cabin, Jim swung toward our beach and slowly sunk into the water, making a perfect landing. I swung back towards our cabin.

"You and Chris put on your life jackets because you're going next!" I called to Mike.

Mike was now thirteen and already a great skier. Chris was only nine, and he had tried several times. Jon threw them the rope, and Chris wrapped his arms around Mike's waist in a crouched position. Everyone was on shore to watch this historic event. Janet and Eric, Chris's older brother, were sitting on the dock. Steve and Kathy were looking on from the shore, and Marilyn and Sandy were sitting on the deck. Doug, Marilyn's oldest son, was helping Mike and Chris stay steady while I picked up the slack in the rope.

"Hit it!" yelled Doug.

I pushed the thrust lever forward, and Mike and Chris popped out of the water. It was a sight for sore eyes. We made a small circle around the middle of the lake watching Mike ski with Chris holding on for dear life.

"Slow it down a little, Tom," yelled Jon with a huge grin on his face as he watched his son on top of the water for the first time.

I gradually swung the boat around and headed back toward the cabin. As I neared the cabin, I gently slowed the boat down, and Mike and Chris sank into the water. Everyone was clapping and cheering. Mike and Chris swam to the shore with big grins on both of their faces.

Janet ran to Chris and gave him a huge hug.

"Now you have the feel for skiing, and I think you can do it alone," she said.

"Can I try it right now, Mom?" asked Chris.

"I think you should rest a little first," Janet responded. "Doug is going to ski now. Maybe you can try it alone after he gets back."

Later that morning, Chris got up alone and felt quite good about his accomplishment. We spent a couple of hours that morning pulling the kids around the lake on water skis. Just before lunch, Jon and Steve decided to go doubles. We loaded up the boat with kids because we all knew they were going to put on a show. Doug, Jim, Mike, and Chris were in the front of the boat. Katie, Eric, Don, and Tim, Don's son, were in the back. I was driving.

Jon and Steve had wide brimmed hats on and looked like circus clowns. I gunned the motor, and they both popped right up. Jon lifted one ski in the air and headed outside the wake looking totally out of control. Steve shot right after him spraying him with water. All the kids were cracking up and going nuts. Jon and Steve swung behind the boat next to each other and began to try to knock each other down. Steve had enough and shot out of the wake with one ski high in the air. Jon just stayed behind the boat. All of a sudden, Jon did a butt drop! He sank down in the water which completely enveloped him. For a moment, all we could see was water. Then, he shot up out of the water waving to us and was skiing bow legged with that silly hat drenched on his head. Both Steve and Jon came together holding hands as I swung the boat by the cabin. They shot into the shore, jumped out of their skis, and ran onto the beach. The kids loved the show. I even put on a smile as I drove back to our shore station.

After a hearty lunch, all the kids and uncles gathered in the backyard for a game of wiffleball. This is a game we loved and played for hours in our backyard. To play wiffleball, you need plastic balls and a plastic bat. Jon was the pitcher, and I was the catcher. He would throw very hard and could make the ball rise, break to the right, or break to the left depending on the type of spin he put on the ball. One by one, the kids batted. They didn't run the bases. A ground ball was an imaginary single, a line drive was a double, and a ball hit to the driveway was a home run. Jon threw the ball toward the cabin, which was used for our backstop. Jon forced all his kids to bat left handed, and they all became good hitters. If the batter hit a ball and it was caught in the air, or if he struck out, another kid would come to the plate. We would all try to see how many imaginary runs we could get. After the kids all took their turns, the uncles would try their hands at it. It was great fun and developed good eye hand coordination in our kids.

After wiffleball, we got up a game of half-court basketball. We played in our driveway where we had a basketball hoop on the garage. We usually played until we could hardly walk. Then, our sweaty bodies made their way to the lake. We ran into the water to refresh in its coolness, unwind, and relax. After that, some of the kids would take out our Sunfish sailboat. The others would just lay on the grass on the front lawn absorbing some sun rays. Needless to say, our days were filled with plenty of activities.

After supper, I prepared the wood for our evening campfire. Our firepit was a deep hole with rocks circled around it. I prepared the teepee style fire with paper, kindling, and logs split into quarters. We would wait for it to get dark before we lit the fire. As darkness settled over the lake, moon beams began shooting across the water, and the stars began to emerge one by one until they lit up the evening sky. The wood would ignite and quickly became a crackling, blazing fire. We gathered lawn chairs around the campfire, and I brought out my guitar. We sang campfire songs, told stories, roasted marshmallows and hot dogs, and ate s'mores.

"Tom, tell us the story about the time you were talking to Sandy on the phone and Jon pulled the chair out from under you," asked Steve.

"They've already heard that story," I responded.

"I haven't heard it," responded Katie.

"Well, back when I was dating Sandy, I was sitting with a blanket over my head talking to her on the phone and leaning back in my chair. Jon walked by and pulled the chair out. I went flying."

"How old were you?" questioned Jim.

"I don't know exactly. I was probably about eighteen or nineteen, and Jon was about fourteen."

"What did you do?" asked Mike.

"What do you think I did? I calmly picked up the phone I had dropped and said, 'Excuse me, Sandy.' Jon shot out the door as I set down the phone and was hot on his heels. I caught him about two blocks later, roughed him up a bit, came back, and continued my conversation as if nothing had happened."

"Did you hurt my dad?" asked Eric.

"Not really. By the time I caught him, I was so tired and out of breath that I didn't have much strength left." I said. "I told him he better never do that again!"

"Mom, tell the story about the time you dropped water on Uncle Steve," yelled Katie.

"Back when your uncles still lived at 4001, your dad gave me a bucket of water and told me to go upstairs and out on the flat roof over the porch. So I did. Your dad yelled to Steve to come outside quick and see something. Steve came running out of the house and said, 'What is it, Tom?'"

Steve shook his head quietly as everyone cracked up.

"He stopped right in front of your dad," Sandy went on. "I unloaded the bucket of water and hit Steve squarely on the head. He was so surprised that he jumped high in the air screaming. It was hilarious, and we all cracked up except for Steve. He didn't think it was so funny! He looked up and saw me with a bucket in my hand. Dripping wet, he looked up at me and said, 'You'll pay for that!'"

"Did you ever get her back, Uncle Steve?" asked Jim.

"No, I don't think so."

"Did I ever tell you about the time I was in the psych ward, and they gave me a test to see if I was nuts?" Don asked.

"No, what happened?" Jon responded laughing.

"Well, they spoke to me in another language and asked me what language they were speaking. How was I supposed to know? Then, they asked me to add two huge numbers together in my head. I told them, 'There isn't a Hall in the world that can answer that question,'" Don stated with a straight face.

"That's the funniest thing I ever heard," Steve roared.

"Then, there was the time my manager was making fun of me for being so short. I just looked at him and said, 'Hey, you're messing with the wrong guy. I'm a giant among midgets,'" Don said with a sly look at Jon and Steve, the short ones in the family.

They glared back at him.

"Tom, tell the story when you did a cartwheel in front of my mom on the beach," suggested Doug.

"Do I have to?" I said blushing.

"Yes!" everyone screamed.

"Marilyn was sitting on the railroad ties that lined the beach. I said, 'Watch this, Marilyn!' I did a cartwheel in my bathing suit, and it split right down the middle. Marilyn cracked up. I quickly dashed into the cabin with a bcet red face and put on another bathing suit."

"Did she see your penis?" asked Katie.

Everyone exploded with laughter!

After our stories were exhausted, the adults continued to talk around the campfire while the cousins played games outside in the dark until about midnight. Totally exhausted, everyone finally headed for their bedrooms. We all crashed into dreamland within a matter of seconds, ending a typical day at the Hall cabin.

DOUG AND JIM

After Dave's death, I had a talk with my brothers one day when were together at the cabin. We were all adults with small children and busy doing life. As we were sitting together on our front lawn, I engaged them in a serious discussion.

"When we're at the cabin, we need to reach out to Doug and Jim," I stated.

"What do you mean?" questioned Jon.

"They don't have a father, so we need to not only be role models but include them in all our activities."

"I agree," added Steve. "We can't be fathers to them, but we should make a special effort to be good uncles."

"What are you suggesting, Tom?" asked Don.

"We just need to make sure that we make a special effort to involve them in whatever activity we're doing. We play a lot of group games around here, like wiffleball, so that shouldn't be hard. Remember, we own this cabin together. It's not just our individual families alone."

"They both like to water ski too," threw in Jon. "Every time we get the boat out, let's make sure they are involved."

As we were talking and brainstorming, we all decided to reach out to Doug and Jim. Our dad had passed away when we were young, so we understood their situation. We all remembered how much we had missed our dad.

Mike and Jim were very close to the same age, so it was quite natural for me to include Jim in all the activities I did with my son. Doug often joined us as well. We spent hours on the lake water skiing, and they all became excellent skiers. Jon was especially good at involving Doug and Jim in everything along with his family. They played many outdoor games together. Whenever we played golf and tennis, we included them as well.

As they grew up, the cousins enjoyed each other without our input or involvement. They would play very intense water games where they would dunk each other in the lake. They would run around the cabin at night playing tag. We also passed on to them our love of card games like cribbage and five hundred. Doug and Jim were always involved.

We enjoyed a lot of half-court basketball together. One time, Doug and I were playing one-on-one. He was quite a bit taller than me and was tough. We got into quite a competitive match, and the game got physical pretty quickly. As I was driving in for a lay-up, Doug moved in to block my shot and accidentally hit my jaw quite hard. I bit through my tongue and had to go to the hospital for stitches. It was quite painful, but Doug definitely had my respect.

It was the cabin that kept us brothers in close contact with Doug and Jim. As they grew up, we all saw qualities of our older brother in both Doug and Jim's lives. I appreciated all of the efforts my brothers took in reaching out to our nephews. We all have a special relationship with them. They both turned out to be great young men, husbands, and fathers. I believe all of those years at the cabin helped them as they grew and matured. Hopefully, we were good role models for those two boys who were missing a great experience with their own father. We all tried our best to make sure they were an important part of our extended family. Doug and Jim both married wonderful wives and are involved with us at the cabin along with their own children.

Unfortunately, I haven't shared much of my feelings about their dad with Doug and Jim. Dave was a great guy and a wonderful big brother. After losing his oldest son, Danny, to leukemia, his faith journey deepened as he turned his life over to Christ. As a teacher and hockey coach, he impacted his students, players, and colleagues in a powerful way. I'm very sad that his life was shortened after forty-two years. We were brothers, colleagues, and very good friends when his life ended. His death greatly impacted my life. Dave was a strong Christian and died trusting Jesus, so I am looking forward to seeing him in heaven someday.

Our cabin was Dave's dream first and became all of our dreams. Thanks to his efforts to get us started, we are living out the reality today. I am grateful to Dave for his vision and action. I also know he would be very proud of his two boys and grandchildren. I love both Doug and Jim and pray for them daily. I want them to know that I would do anything for them.

CRISIS AT THE CABIN

"Tom, answer the door," yelled Sandy from the kitchen.

I opened the front door, and a man dressed in a suit was holding a registered letter addressed to me. I had to sign my name before he would give it to me.

"Sandy, you have to see this letter I just received," I called.

She came into the living room and saw the unopened letter I was holding in my hand.

"What is it, Tom?" she asked.

"It's a certified letter, but I'm not really sure what it's all about."

"Open it, Tom!"

I opened it and began reading silently. Sandy tried to read the expression on my face.

"What is it, Tom? You look so serious. You're scaring me."

"It's from Don's attorney."

Don had been having financial problems. He hadn't made any lake payments for over ten years. It was getting to be a real issue, and my family wanted me to confront him about his struggle. However, this letter would force us all into action.

I gave the letter to Sandy, who read it carefully. After she read it, she gave it back to me and was silent for a period of time.

"What do you think it means?" I questioned.

"Evidently, Don got into financial trouble with his attorney. When Don couldn't pay him his fees, he asked Don if he had any collateral. Don said that he was a part owner in a lake home in Wisconsin with his brothers. He had Don sign some papers, and now we have a new owner. Don has given this guy his share of the cabin."

"I can't believe Don would do this!" I exclaimed. "I can't believe this attorney would take advantage of Don like this! What are we going to do?"

"We'll need to contact Marilyn, Bob, Jon, and Steve to see if they got this same certified letter. It seems this sleezeball wants us to auction off our cabin, and he would receive one sixth of the profit."

"Can he do that?" I asked.

"Well, we have to appear in court on April 5, 1995 to decide the fate of our cabin," responded Sandy.

I was angry with Don. What was he thinking anyway? I knew it wouldn't do any good to confront Don. He had gone through a tough divorce and wasn't healthy. Just the same, his struggles had affected the entire family. Now, we had to fight for our cabin. I wasn't sure what to do.

"Sandy, this cabin means so much to our family. It was Dave's vision and God's gift to us. It's what will keep our family together, and now it may tear us apart. I'm not sure what to do."

"We're not in this alone. We need to talk it over with everyone before we decide what course of action to take."

"I'd like to pray and ask the Lord to help us," I said. "Dear Father, You have been with our family and seen us through some very difficult times. You have blessed us with our beautiful lake home. Now, it seems we have a new partner who wants us to sell it at an auction and divide up the profits. We need your direction and wisdom. Please don't let this attorney get away with this. Please be with Don. Help him recover from his struggle, and help us not to be angry with him. Thank you! In Jesus' name, amen."

I called my brothers and Marilyn. Each of them also received a summons to appear in court on April 5th. Bob was even summoned in New York City. We decided we would go to the courthouse together. Sandy also would join Jon, Steve, and I because she had been taking care of all the financial records for our cabin. Marilyn decided not to attend the court hearing, and Bob could not be there as well.

Don's attorney had our cabin appraised, so we hired an appraiser as well. I met him at our cabin and walked through it with him. I tried to point out all the things that were wrong and hoped he would appraise the cabin low. He valued our cabin at $112,000. I don't know the value of the attorney's appraisal.

We also had to hire a Wisconsin attorney. I had a good friend who was an outstanding attorney, so I called him up. He recommended a friend from law school who was a sharp guy and would do well for us. He was a wise attorney. So, I called him, gave him the facts, and sent him the certified letter. We retained his services, and he agreed to represent us in court on April 5th. We had several phone conversations, and Sandy and I drove to his Wisconsin office to talk with him. We were both confident that he was the right man to represent us.

On the morning of April 5th, Jon and Steve drove over to my house at 7:30 AM. The court time was 10:30 to determine the fate of our cabin. We stopped for breakfast on the way to Siren, Wisconsin. We didn't really know what to expect, and we didn't know if Don would be in court or not. During breakfast, we had a discussion concerning our court battle and expectations.

"I've never been through anything like this, Tom. What do you think will happen?" asked Steve.

"We have our attorney, and they will have theirs. Don's attorney is from Minnesota, so I think he will need to hire a Wisconsin attorney as well," I responded.

"Do you think they will put us on the stand?" asked Jon.

"They might. If they do, just answer the questions honestly. I'm sure they will put Sandy on the stand because she has all the records of our finances. She has meticulously kept excellent records of all our spending and how much Don is behind and owes us. I'm sure these records will help our cause. Jon, would you pray for a positive outcome of this hearing?" I requested.

"Sure, Tom," Jon responded.

Right there in the middle of the restaurant, we all bowed our heads, closed our eyes, and listened to Jon's prayer.

"Dear Father," Jon prayed. "I pray that you will be present at this hearing. I pray that you would give our attorney wisdom and insight as he fights for us. I pray that the judge would give us a fair settlement. Please, Father, allow us to keep our cabin so our families can enjoy it for years to come. Help us be open and honest if we are put on the stand. And please give Sandy wisdom, clarity, and insight. Thank you for hearing our prayer and keeping our family close. In Jesus' name, amen."

As we neared the courthouse, my stomach began to churn. I had the butterflies just like I did before a hockey game. We entered the courthouse and were directed to a room. We met our attorney and sat with him in the front row. Don's attorney sat across the aisle with his attorney from Wisconsin. Don wasn't there.

A man walked into the courtroom and told us all to rise. Then, the judge dressed in a black robe entered the courtroom.

"You may be seated," she said sitting down at her bench.

She had already been briefed on the case. The attorneys each made their opening remarks and then argued back and forth for a while. One attorney would make a statement, and the other would respond. The judge called for the first witness. Sandy was called to the front and, with her hand on the Bible, took the oath to tell the whole truth. Our attorney asked her about how we handled being multiple owners. She responded by saying we each contributed a monthly fee and shared all the expenses. She also mentioned that Don had not been able to make his payments for over ten years.

After our attorney was finished questioning Sandy, their attorney cross examined her. He began by asking her questions about certain finances. Sandy had documented answers for each question. During the dialogue, Sandy mentioned how we came from a poor family and had saved money as children to purchase this property. He responded by telling her to just answer the question.

As he continued to question Sandy, she was able to tell the story of how we were able to acquire the land and build this cabin as a family. I was watching as the judge listened intently to her responses on each question. I glanced across the aisle and overheard Don's attorney whisper.

"Stop questioning this witness. She is too well prepared."

After Sandy's brilliant performance, the judge asked if us brothers would like to come to the stand. We looked at each other and shook our heads.

"No, Your Honor," I responded.

The judge then dismissed us, and we walked out to the lobby. Our attorney came and talked to us.

"I'm encouraged by what just happened in court," he said. "The judge is going over all the information and will make a settlement. She will then call both attorneys and give us her decision. Sandy, you were great on the stand. I think you greatly impacted the judge's decision."

Then, our attorney walked over and shook the hand of the opposing attorney. I was amazed the way they treated and respected one another. When they were in court, they seemed so hostile to one another. I guess it's just a game they play.

A decision was rendered after about an hour. Our attorney came over and went over the document with us. He was amazed at how low the settlement came in considering the worth of our cabin. We only had to pay a small amount of money to Don's attorney, so that he could pay his attorney. I'm sure he saw dollar signs when he became a part owner of our cabin. I'm sure it didn't turn out the way he planned. We thanked our attorney for his fine representation and drove home.

On the way home we discussed the court hearing in the car.

"I was nervous when we entered the courtroom," I stated.

"I thought Don would be there," threw in Jon.

"Our attorney did an outstanding job when questioning Sandy," responded Steve.

"Sandy, you were great answering his questions. But, you really shined when their attorney cross examined you," stated Jon.

"Were you nervous, Hon?" I questioned.

"I was a little nervous at first. But, I had everything documented, and the questions were easy. I just really wanted the judge to hear how you boys saved to build this cabin since you were children."

"You really won the judge over to our side when you explained how we saved our change to buy the land," commented Steve.

"Yes, and also when you told her how we built our first cabin with our own bare hands," added Jon.

"Their attorney was digging himself into a hole when he kept asking questions. You let the judge know that Don hadn't paid his share for years and made his attorney look like he was taking advantage of Don's struggle," I threw in.

"Sandy, we all owe you big time. You just saved our cabin. Thank you for your great organization and beautiful performance under oath today. You could have won an Academy Award!" exclaimed Jon.

During the next week, we had to take out a loan in order to pay our bill to their attorney and ours. Our cabin had been almost paid off. Now, we had another big loan to deal with. Thankfully, our payments were manageable. Don was no longer a part owner, and neither was his attorney. We were all very grateful we didn't have to sell our cabin or put it up for auction. It would remain in our family.

During this time, I talked with Bob and had asked him how he felt about owning the cabin and not being able to contribute any support.

"Tom, I think you should take my name off the cabin," he said. "I live in New York, and my children live here as well. I think it would be better if my name was not on the cabin. It could get messy with our children, and I don't want them to go through all that."

"Bob, I think you are right. I want you to know that you and your family will always be welcome and specifically have a week up there."

Bob's name was also taken off the title by our attorney. That left Marilyn, Jon, Steve, and me as owners. Thus, we averted a crisis and continued to have this summer place to enjoy as a family.

MY CHILDREN AT THE CABIN

Our summers at the cabin were always fantastic. We had many options, and we used them all. We fished off the dock and used all our boats to search the lake for the big ones. We sailed on the Sunfish sailboat, played half-court basketball, pitched horseshoes, went swimming, water skied, and played badminton and wiffleball. There also was a tennis court nearby, and a golf course was just fifteen minutes away. We basically played from morning to night, going from one activity to another. In the evening, we usually had a campfire with stories, singing and deep conversation.

As our families grew up, our children joined in and played hard with us brothers. Our family grew close, and the cousins pretty much grew up together at the cabin during the summers. They became lifelong friends. My brother's dream had come true. We had a place we could be proud of, and I'm sorry he didn't see the final results of his creative efforts.

Maybe, he did. Our dad would have loved to see this place and our family interacting as well.

The cabin had a strong impact on my two children, Mike and Katie. They both gained confidence and endurance as a result of the many activities we enjoyed together. I watched them grow in character and was blessed to enjoy many wonderful times with them at the cabin.

My son, Mike, always loved the water and spent much time swimming in our lake as a little boy. He became a good swimmer as a result of our times at the cabin.

Doug came to me one time with a request.

"Tom, I want to swim across the lake. Will you follow me in the canoe?"

"Sure!" I responded heading to grab a paddle.

Mike overheard what Doug had said to me. When I returned with the paddle, Mike had his own question for me.

"Can I swim across the lake too, Dad?"

I gazed across the lake and questioned myself concerning Mike's request. Mike was only in fourth grade, and Doug was in ninth grade.

"I know I can do it, Dad! Please give me a chance!" he said.

Reluctantly, I consented. I got out our Grumman canoe, threw in two extra life jackets, and pushed out into the lake. Doug and Mike waded into the water, and both dove in at the same time.

"Doug, I want you to stay with Mike," I said. "You may need to slow down from time to time because you're bigger and stronger. I have life jackets with me. If you get tired or need help, just yell and I'll throw you a jacket."

So, Mike and Doug set out on what I call an endurance swim. It was about three-quarters of a mile across the lake. They both took it easy. When they got tired, they would turn over and float on their backs to catch their wind. Through hard work and determination, they made it to the other side. Mike was pretty tired.

"Tom, I want to swim back," stated Doug.

"So do I!" responded Mike.

"I'm sure Doug can make it back, but I don't know if you have the strength, Son," I said with a concerned look on my face.

"Dad, please give me the chance. If I need help, you can throw me a life jacket."

Once again, I reluctantly consented. Mike and Doug swam together until we got to the middle of the lake.

"Tom, I feel fine," Doug said. "I want to motor in."

He took off without waiting to hear my response. Mike continued to stroke and rest periodically. I paddled next to him and kept a close eye on Doug as well. He seemed to reach the shore with ease.

"How are you doing, Son?" I called from the canoe.

"I'm a little tired, but I feel okay," Mike replied.

"Let me know if you need any help, alright?"

"I will, Dad. Just keep going."

So, that little ten year old son of mine kept stroking and watched his destination get closer and closer. When he made it to shore and could stand up, he just looked at me as if to say, "I told you so, Dad." No words needed to be expressed. I saw that little smile of satisfaction and realized that a milestone had been completed in his life. That determination would be one of his great character qualities as he moved into his adult life. At the cabin, my son matured, grew in character, and gained confidence.

Mike watched his father and uncles water ski from a young age. As a result, he was greatly motivated to learn to water ski. When he was eight years old, he began his journey. We had a small pair of red wooden water skis that he used. Getting up was not easy, and Mike fell again and again. However, he was determined and wouldn't quit. Finally, he popped up behind the boat, and I took him in a small circle. This success was all he needed. Mike wanted to ski all the time, so I spent many hours pulling him all over the lake. He couldn't get enough. When Mike was in his junior year of high school, we bought him an outstanding slalom ski with its own case. He prized this possession and still has it. As Mike got older, I began to help him take his skiing to the next level.

"When you ski, you're playing it too safe," I said. "I want you to extend your arms and deepen your cuts. I know you can do it."

"If I do that, Dad, I will fall!" he said.

"If you aren't falling, you're not cutting deep enough. You should lean out and almost touch your shoulder to the water. I'd also like to see you cut equally well on both sides of the wake."

Mike took the challenge. As he started to stretch himself, he fell often but always got back up determined to do better. As he improved, he wouldn't bail out on his cuts. He had a certain speed he liked, which was thirty-seven miles per hour.

Mike's skiing was something to behold. One time, he decided to start his ski run with a flying dock start. He stood about ten feet back from the edge of the dock with the ski on his left foot and a few feet of rope coiled in his right hand. I brought the boat into position.

"Hit it!" he yelled when he was ready.

I slammed down the throttle. When the rope tightened, Mike hopped about three times on the dock while holding the ski on his left foot up and keeping its tip pointed up. When he came to the end of the dock, he threw the coil of rope into the air and flew off the dock. He sailed out about ten feet and landed in the water perfectly. Mike's performance was spectacular. He relaxed in the middle of the wake with perfect form. When the boat reached calm water, Mike began his cuts. He swung out to the left holding the handle of the rope with both hands and made a deep cut in the water. At the point of his turn, his body was almost horizontal with the surface of the water, and a huge spray shot up over his head. He then shot back across the wake and made the same cut on the right side. Mike's cuts were so deep that they actually impacted the boat. He could cut on a dime and leave eight cents' change.

Mike skied to the point of exhaustion. When that happened, he pointed his thumb over his left shoulder, and I headed for the cabin. On the way back, he held the handle of the rope with his arm bent at the elbow and just relaxed in the middle of the wake. Mike put on a show with his landing as well. He made a wide swing, glided to shore, and casually stepped out of his ski. As I put the boat back into the shore station, I saw a little smile on his face. It had been a good run.

Slalom skiing was not our only water sport. We had a small ski about a foot long called the Ski-Skat. Mike was really good with it. Whenever he used it, he really kicked up a wake. We also had a kneeboard, and everyone enjoyed using it. It was shaped like a surfboard but was a lot smaller. It had two retractable fins which stabilized the board and enabled the rider to cut across the wake. To use it, a person would lie on his stomach holding the handle in front of the tip of the kneeboard. I would push the boat throttle just to move fast enough to get the tip up. With the tip out of the water, the rider would slowly pull himself up until he was kneeling on the board. Finally, he would wrap a belt across his knees and swing in and out of the wake.

After a while, this was not much of a challenge, so we retracted the fins. This made the bottom of the board smooth. At first, it was a real challenge to go sideways, but the kids figured it out. Then, Mike figured out how to grab the rope behind his back and spin around in a complete circle. Peer pressure was obvious. Most of the cousins eventually learned to do a series of circles in either direction.

One day, I came up with the ultimate challenge.

"I heard someone say that it was possible to ski on a canoe paddle," I said.

"How could anyone ski on a canoe paddle?" questioned Mike.

"Well, from what I heard, you have to get up on two skis. One is a regular ski, and the other is a canoe paddle. The rider has to bend over and hold the end of the paddle in his hand. The long handle acts as a rudder. When the boat is moving, the force of the water keeps the paddle on his foot. Slowly, the rider stands up, drops the ski, and slides the empty foot behind the first foot on the canoe paddle."

"Wow!" stated Mike. "That seems impossible!"

Everyone wanted to attempt this feat. Mike was the first to try. In the process of getting up, he snapped the paddle. All the boys tried. Time after time, each of them failed. We broke a few more paddles in the process.

Finally, it was Katie's turn. She was the only girl among all of her boy cousins. No one gave her much of a chance. She was thirteen years old at his time in her life and was a lot lighter than all her boy cousins. This was to her advantage.

Katie jumped into the water with all the confidence of a Navy SEAL. She had a huge smile on her face and no fear. She was determined. She put on one ski and held the canoe paddle with her left hand.

"Drag me slowly, Dad, and I'll keep the tips up. Then, when I stand up, give me a little more speed."

"Okay, Babe!" I yelled back.

Katie began her run with all the boys anxiously watching her. She was determined to do something none of the boys could do. Bending over in a crouched position, she slowly stood up and dropped her ski. Very carefully, she placed her right foot behind her left foot and leaned back. The long handle of the paddle served as a rudder. A huge wave gushed up over her head making her invisible to those of us in the boat. All we could see was someone totally immersed in water. To everyone's amazement, Katie remained on that canoe paddle for the entire run. I swung the boat around and headed back for the cabin. To rub in her accomplishment a little more, she came into shore on that paddle for a perfect landing. To this day, no one has matched her experience. That display of skill and determination made that exercise a legend at our cabin. I learned to never underestimate my daughter. Katie was and still is tenacious just like me.

One time a few years later, our family was alone at the cabin. Mike was not with us, so it was just Sandy, Katie and me. After breakfast and a refreshing swim, Katie had a suggestion.

"Dad, let's take out the canoe and paddle around the perimeter of the lake," she said. "Let's take our time and just enjoy each other."

"That sounds like a great idea," I answered.

I headed for the garage and got the paddles and cushions for the seats. The cushions also served as life preservers.

"Sandy, Katie and I are taking the canoe out and paddling around the perimeter of the lake. We'll be gone for most of the day," I stated walking down to the lake.

"Tom, it's cloudy and might rain. I haven't heard a weather report. You could get stranded at the far end of the lake, and a hailstorm could come up."

"Sandy, the lake isn't that big. We are both strong paddlers. If a storm comes up, we'll stroke directly back to the cabin. We will never be more than a half hour away."

"Be careful, Tom," Sandy warned.

"We will. If you're worried, say a prayer for us. This is a great time for Katie and me. We should be back around 4:30 or 5:00."

So, off we went slowly stroking together. We headed along the west shoreline traveling south. Everything appeared more beautiful from the canoe. We were used to seeing things pass by so quickly in our speedboat. Now, we had a great chance to study the incredible scenery around the lake at our slow pace. Both Katie and I were good paddlers as we had spent time in the Boundary Waters together.

As Katie was paddling in the bow, I noticed her strong shoulders, athletic body, and beautiful long brown hair. She was not a little girl anymore. She had become a beautiful young woman, and I was so proud of her.

When we reached the point, just four cabins away from ours, the shoreline swung around and formed a bay with calm crystal blue water. Many beautiful trees lined the shoreline.

"Dad, look up at the maple tree!" yelled Katie.

"Where?"

"The huge one right next to the cabin on the point."

"Oh, yeah! I see it!"

Perched on one of the higher branches was a spectacular bald eagle.

"What a magnificent bird, Dad!" Katie exclaimed.

Just then, it took off and circled high above us with another eagle. They must have been mates. The two eagles hooked their talons together and started tumbling toward the lake. Just before they reached the lake, they unclasped and flew off into the distant horizon.

"Wow! That was quite a show, Dad!"

"You got that right, Babe!" I exclaimed.

As we stroked around the bay, we came to the channel leading to the back bay where we had built our first cabin.

"Let's paddle into the back bay and see our old cabin from the lake," stated Katie.

"Sounds like a plan," I said.

I dug my paddle into the water and turned the canoe down the middle of the channel. The channel was narrow and very shallow. There were lily pads and bull rushes all along the shoreline. On our right, we noticed the point where our peninsula ended. As we entered the back bay, we observed a much different atmosphere. A water pathway stretched down the middle of the bay. Tall weeds were sticking up out of the water on each side of it. The water was shallow and filled with lily pads and weeds. We paddled down the water path until we came to the spot where our old cabin was located. We stroked through the weeds, came right in front of our old cabin, and stared at it from the water.

"Looks different from out here, doesn't it, Babe?" I said.

We observed the boathouse built into the side of the hill. To the right of the boathouse were the railroad tie steps we had created. The same stately Norway pines stood on top of the hill. Nestled in between the trees was the cabin we had built with its flat roof and windows facing the lake.

"We sure had a lot of fun growing up there, Dad," Katie said.

"Yes, we did. You were just eight years old when we sold it and moved to the other side of the peninsula."

"It was much more wooded here than on our new lot. We would play hide and seek in the trees. Sometimes, I would even stand like a statue. When it was really dark, my cousins would walk right past me."

"How was it growing up with all boy cousins?" I questioned.

"I had to learn to be tough. I think it helped me when I got older, especially in sports."

"You are quite an athlete, Katie," I said proudly. "You're involved in tennis, basketball, and track."

"It's a lot of work, but I love it. What do you expect from a daughter of yours?" Katie asked.

"I'm very proud of you, but I would be just as proud of you if you weren't involved in any sports."

"Come on, Dad! You love to watch my tennis matches, my basketball games, and my running."

"I love it when you get that fire in your eyes, just like your old man."

We paddled back to the channel. In the middle of the channel, we saw a small waterway heading towards another bay. We called it Hidden River.

"We'll have to take that some other day. I hear there is a big beaver lodge in that bay, but it's difficult to canoe to because of the heavy vegetation on the lake," I commented.

We got back into the big portion of Sand Lake and paddled along the shoreline talking and looking at all the cabins. It was during the week, so the cabins were empty. We owned the lake.

"What's that in the water, Dad?"

We canoed over to the spot Katie indicated and saw a huge walleye on its side struggling for life.

"That is a huge fish. It must have been injured or something," I said.

We continued paddling. Suddenly, an eagle swooped down from the sky, grabbed the walleye in its talons, and flew right over our heads.

"Wow! That eagle is performing for us, Daddy," Katie said.

As we continued on in our journey, I noticed a newly constructed cabin being built high off the water in dense woods.

"Let's check out the newly constructed cabin," I suggested angling the canoe toward the shoreline.

"Won't we get nailed for trespassing?" questioned Katie a little concerned.

"No one's around. I would just like to investigate a fancy looking lake home," I responded.

We beached our canoe, trudged up a ton of stairs, and faced a beautiful lake home with steep peaks and enormous windows facing the lake. We walked into the home and toured the building. It had a gorgeous view, a beautiful stone fireplace, and two levels with large rooms.

"It looks like something you would see in the movies," noted Katie.

"Some architect had fun designing this home. It's gorgeous!" I answered.

"I wonder what it cost to design and build this home," Katie said.

"As beautiful as it is, I wouldn't trade our cabin for this one."

"Why not, Dad?"

"We have a better lot, and we're right on the water. Our beach is much nicer, and our cabin fits our family better."

After exploring the newly constructed lake home, we walked down the steps and back to our canoe. We continued our journey until we came to a floating dock. I pulled the canoe alongside the dock.

"It's time to get wet!" I yelled.

"Dad, we can't just play on someone else's dock!" Katie said rather shocked.

"Why not?" I responded.

I climbed on to the aluminum dock. It was carpeted and had a diving board on one end. I ran to the end of the dock and did a swan dive deep into the cool, clear, blue water of Sand Lake. As I emerged from the water, I realized Katie was right behind me.

"What a rush!" she yelled as she popped up right next to me.

"It doesn't get any better than this," I yelled climbing up for another dive.

We dove and swam at that lovely dock for about thirty minutes before getting back into our canoe to travel forward and onward. We came to an inlet that led to Thompson Bay. The water there was very shallow. On entering the bay, which was completely blocked from sight in the larger lake, we noticed very nicely built homes around the semicircle of the bay. As we were paddling, I glanced into the water and observed a swarm of small sunnies.

"Look at all those fish!" yelled Katie. "Too bad we don't have our fishing rods, Dad!"

"It's okay," I said. "This is not a fishing trip anyway. It's an 'enjoy my little girl' trip."

"No, it's an 'enjoy my big, strong, masculine father' trip."

We paddled out of the bay and headed down the east side of the lake directly opposite from our cabin. There wasn't much sandy beach on this side of the lake. All the cabins were high off the lake with big stairways leading down to the water. We noticed all the varieties of cabins. Then, we swung into a little cove to see The Brown Jug, one of the two restaurants on our lake.

"I would offer to buy you lunch, but since I'm just in my swimsuit and without my billfold, we'd have to do dishes to pay the bill."

"It's okay, Dad. Even though I'm a little hungry, I can wait until we get home."

"Do you want to paddle back across the lake to the cabin and get some lunch?"

"No. I want to continue until we've paddled the entire perimeter of our lake. We started something, Dad, and I want to finish it!"

We continued on our journey around the cove and came to a lovely cabin on a high hill overlooking the lake. It had a great view and about three hundred feet of lakeshore. As we turned the corner, we saw an airplane sitting on a platform on the shoreline.

"So, this is where that plane lives," stated Katie. "How do they get it on that platform?"

As we paddled closer, we spied metal tracks under water.

"Look at those tracks, Katie. The platform rolls out to the plane. Somehow, the plane is hoisted onto that round platform. Then, it is driven electrically to the shoreline."

"Pretty cool, Dad. Wouldn't it be nice to fly up here like that?"

"It would. However, it's only a two hour drive for us, so that's not too bad."

As we came to the north shore of the lake, we observed a series of smaller cabins that looked like they had been added on to.

"How come all those cabins look the same?" asked Katie.

"This used to be The Sand Bar Resort. All those cabins were part of the resort. When the resort went out of business, the cabins were sold off individually. People bought them and added their own touch to them. Notice the beautiful sandy beaches in front of each cabin. The only problem with these cabins is that the lots are very small, and they are located right on busy County Road A."

Near the end of these homes, we saw a sign for The Sand Bar. This was the other restaurant on the lake. We had often eaten there or ordered pizzas for dinner. We also drove our speedboat there to buy gas. Both Katie and I were familiar with The Sand Bar.

As we rounded the north end of the lake and headed down the west shore, we sighted many small cabins next to very large lake homes.

"At one time, all the cabins on this like were like those little ones," I stated.

"What happened to all the smaller cabins, Dad?"

"Rich people bought them, tore them down, and built nice lake homes."

"Where did they get all their money?"

"I don't know, but some people seem to have an endless supply."

We were on the last leg of our journey and had been gone a long time. We paddled past the boat landing and kept admiring the beautiful homes.

"Katie, you have one year left of school. What are your future plans?" I asked.

"I want to go to college and be a teacher like you, Dad. I think I'll go to Saint Cloud State," she said.

"Are you sure you want to be a teacher?"

"At least for a while. I really want to be a mom and have a family."

"Do you want a big family?"

"Not too big, maybe three or four kids. I hope I can stay home and be a full-time mom, just like Mom!"

"It's hard for me to accept the fact that you're almost fully grown and will leave home shortly. I don't know if I'm ready for that."

"That's life, Dad. But, I have a feeling that wherever I live, we'll always be close."

"You, Katie, unlike your friends, have never been ashamed of me. You've always wanted me around."

"That's because my friends think you are cool! And you know something? They're right!"

"I see our cabin just around the bend. Let's lean on our paddles because I'm really getting hungry."

So, Katie and I turned on the afterburners, leaving a wake behind our canoe. In no time at all, we were in front of our cabin.

"We made a lifetime memory today, Daddy. I'll never forget this day."

"Neither will I, Babe. Neither will I!" I responded.

When my son, Mike, graduated from high school, he was accepted into the United States Air Force

Academy. Just before he was to report to Colorado Springs for his basic training, we decided to make a last trip to the cabin in June. He wanted his cousin, Jim, to be up there with him. We called Jim, and he was available to come with us. Mike, Jim, and I spent a couple of days at the cabin together. We had a good time playing golf, swimming, and water skiing.

Just before we decided to travel home, Jim and Mike wanted to make a last water ski run. There was no one on the lake as they sped up and down the shoreline pulling one another. Both of them were amazing on the water. In the meantime, I was cutting the grass. As they pulled the boat into our shore station, I noticed a car pull into our driveway. A man in uniform approached me.

"Do you live here?" he questioned as he approached.

"Yes, I do. Is there a problem?" I asked.

"There is. I would like to talk to the two young men who have been water skiing," he responded.

He walked around to the front of the cabin as Jim was getting out of the boat. Mike was still in the water and hid behind our boat as the man approached Jim.

"May I speak to you?" he stated as he approached Jim. "Where is your friend?"

"He's still in the water," stated Jim turning toward the water. "Mike, come on up here. This gentleman would like to talk to us."

Mike was nervous because he was leaving to report to the Air Force Academy in just a week and didn't want anything on his record. Reluctantly, Mike pulled himself onto the dock and stood beside Jim facing the DNR officer.

"You boys were skiing illegally," he said. "You did not have a spotter in your boat. You also came too close to the docks. You must always ski at least a hundred feet from the docks by the shoreline."

"How did you know how close we came to the docks?" Jim asked as Mike stood next to him with a worried expression on his face.

"I was watching you in my car with binoculars. I am going to have to write you boys up. The fine will be eighty-five dollars," he said as he began writing out the ticket. "You will need to pay immediately, or I will have to take you to jail."

I came out to the dock to see what the commotion was all about.

"Dad, do you have any cash on you?" asked Mike. "We need to pay an eighty-five dollar fine or be arrested."

"I don't have that much cash on me," I responded.

"Will you take a credit card?" responded Jim.

"That will work," answered the officer.

He wrote out a citation and handed it to Jim. Jim gave him his credit card. The officer went back to his car and wrote out a receipt. When he came back from his car, he handed Jim the receipt.

"Make sure you obey the rules. Always have a spotter and ski further out in the lake," he stated firmly.

As he walked back to his car, we just gazed at each other in silence for a while.

"I'll pay our half of the fine next week," I told Jim.

"Thanks, Jim, for handling that situation. I wasn't sure what to do and was very nervous about having a ticket on my record. That could jeopardize my chances of being accepted at the Air Force Academy," stated Mike.

"I can't believe he sits in his car and scans the lake with his binoculars when no one is on the lake," I stated. "Just the same, we need to always have a spotter and stay at least a hundred feet away from the docks."

After that incident, we packed up and went home. The officer had pretty much spoiled Mike's last weekend at the lake. He was just doing his job, and we were breaking the law. So, there wasn't much we could do about the whole situation.

The next weekend, I drove Mike to the airport and said good-bye as he boarded the plane. As I drove home, I had a hollow empty feeling in my stomach. Mike and I were very close, and a good-bye in his eighteenth year was just too sudden and abrupt. He would be gone for four years at school, and then he would serve time in the Air Force. I realized that my parenting for him was pretty much over. I parked the car and went for a long walk. I couldn't help feeling sad and helpless. I wondered how Mike would do and what our role as parents would be like now that our son had left home. Little did I know what was in store for us.

THE BUNKHOUSE

Our new cabin was completed in 1980. Today, our family continues to enjoy the cabin. Our children have grown up, and now our grandkids are sharing our experiences.

Since the cabin was built, we have done several maintenance projects. We put on new front and back decks and repainted the outside of the cabin two times. We tore off the original roof and re-roofed it ourselves. Even just the normal upkeep has kept us busy. We also had to recarpet and paint the inside of our cabin and replace the linoleum in the bathrooms, kitchen, and dining area with ceramic tile.

As our extended family continued to grow, we began running out of space. Our children have gotten married and now have children of their own. We began to feel a need to expand to have more room for all of us. We were at the cabin one weekend discussing this situation and trying to come up with a solution. It was after dinner as all the owners were sitting in the living room. Janet and Kathy had dished us up some dessert, and Marilyn had put on a fresh pot of coffee.

"What do you all think of a bunkhouse for the kids to sleep in?" I suggested.

"Where are you going to put it?" asked Janet.

"On the north side of the lot, maybe," I countered.

"I don't think a bunkhouse is a good idea," replied Janet.

"How about adding on to the garage," suggested Jon.

"How would we do that?" responded Steve.

"We'd hire a carpenter and add a sleeping area next to the garage," replied Jon.

"Where are we going to get the money to do that?" questioned Sandy.

"We'd have to take out a loan," he answered.

"We can't afford any higher payments," commented Sandy as several others nodded their heads in agreement.

"Interest rates are down. We could probably get a fixed thirty year loan which would not increase our payments," stated Janet.

"Why don't you look into a loan for us, Janet?" I suggested.

After this discussion, Janet was commissioned to look into a loan. I decided to contact Wayne Nutt, who was an outstanding builder in the area. He had a good reputation and was reasonable.

The next week, I invited Wayne Nutt to our cabin. When he came over, Jon, Steve, Doug, Marilyn's oldest son, and I had a talk with him. We explained that we wanted to add on to our garage.

"Ideally, what would you like?" he asked us.

"Well, there are four families who own this property. If you could build us each a room and a small family room, that would be great," I suggested.

"Why don't you sketch out what you would like? Send it to me, and I'll see what I can do," Wayne said. "The DNR doesn't like to build too much on a lot.".

During the next week, Sandy sketched out a floor plan adding onto our garage and sent it to Wayne. He sent it back and said it couldn't be done. He suggested we tear down the garage and start over. He included a rough sketch of what we could do with a new garage with storage. Using Wayne's sketch and total measurements, Sandy made modifications and changes that could work for our family. There would be no water, toilets, or kitchen. Sandy sketched out the changes to scale on graph paper and sent it back to Wayne. After looking it over, Wayne called and said it was workable.

"Hi, Tom. The sketch your wife sent me is workable, I should be able to do it for you. Now, I'll need to get a permit."

"Let's do it, then! Let me know what happens." I said.

"I'll submit it tomorrow."

"Thanks, Wayne. I hope it works out. We would really like to do this project with you at the helm."

"Thanks, Tom. I hope it works out too," he said.

About a week later, Wayne called and said the permit was approved. We discussed tearing down the old garage. Wayne offered to do that for us at a reasonable price. That summer, Wayne and his son and a crew of two brothers worked on our new project. They tore down the garage. Wayne was able to use the old cement slab, which was still in good condition. He added to the cement slab doing the concrete work himself.

In about four weeks, we had a new garage with a family room and one large bedroom downstairs and three smaller rooms upstairs. Wayne did the wiring and all the work except taping the drywall and the ceilings. He hired a very professional man from Frederic to do that job.

We helped Wayne with some of the projects like staining the trim and painting the outside and inside to save money. Steve, Jim, and I sprayed the inside walls one weekend while the girls drove into town, picked out some carpet, and hired a carpet layer to install it. The following weekend, we all painted the outside of the bunkhouse. We rented a paint sprayer from Ace Hardware in Webster. A year earlier, we had bought a fiberglass storage shed to store our lawn mowers, gasoline, tools, and other garage materials. That gave us lots of room to store our boat over the winter.

When the project was completed, Wayne took us on a tour. We call this beautiful building our bunkhouse. Everything looked great, except for one minor point.

"Wayne, I want some more outlets in my room," Janet stated.

He sighed, shrugged his shoulders, and complied.

We drew straws to see who would get which room. We all decided to give Marilyn the large downstairs room because it would be difficult for her to climb the steep stairs. Steve got the larger upstairs room, and Jon and I got the smaller rooms. We now had four more rooms to go with the five bedrooms in our cabin. Each family has two rooms, and we have one guest room in the main cabin which anyone can use and Bob gets when he comes.

Sandy and I found a banker in Webster who worked out a loan for our four families. He actually came over to our cabin, and we all signed the loan papers there. Our payments didn't increase, and we were all happy with the finances. However, it is now a thirty year mortgage, so we'll be paying again for a long time.

"Let's work on the landscaping," suggested Kathy as we were sitting on the deck late one Saturday afternoon.

"That sounds like a great idea," answered Janet sitting next to Kathy on the bench glider.

"What can we do with the landscaping?" I questioned.

"First of all, we need to get rid of that overgrown arborvitae tree next to the cabin and that ugly plant in front of it. It looks terrible and is an eye sore," Kathy commented.

"I agree," answered Jon getting up from the table.

"Where are you going, Jon?" I asked.

"I'm going to get the come-along and pull down that tree."

"You mean you want to begin the landscaping project right now?" questioned Steve.

"Why not? We can't do anything until we remove those ugly plants."

That's how many projects began at the cabin. They would begin with a normal conversation. Before anyone knew it, we were working. Jon came back from the garage with the come-along motor, Steve had an ax, and I had branch clippers to cut branches. Jon wrapped wires around the arborvitae tree and hooked the motor to another tree. Steve began digging and chopping roots, and I was cutting branches. After the motor and steel wire was wrapped around an ash tree, Jon hooked it up to a battery and turned up the juice. The tree bent under the pressure from the steel wire, but the root system was too strong for it to budge.

"Keep chopping those roots, Steve, because it's beginning to move!" encouraged Jon.

All of a sudden, the roots gave way, and the tree fell to the ground. We pulled out the large, over-grown shrub the same way. We then cut up all the branches and threw them behind our garage. We would later burn them up. We raked up the debris, filled in the holes with sand, and were now ready for some serious landscaping.

The next weekend, we came up with bullet shaped bricks to outline and edge in our shrubs. We brought brown matting to line the ground to pre-vent weeds and wood chips for ground cover. Becky, Mike's wife, and I began to line up the bullet bricks on the ground.

"How are you going to arrange those bricks in the ground?" questioned Janet standing on the deck looking down at us.

"I thought we'd just make a straight line and close it in on the ends," I answered.

"You can't do that! It would look stupid," Janet said marching down the steps on a mission.

She made a curved line using our hose in the grass.

"Follow this line with the bullets, and it will look much nicer."

"I'm glad I thought of that!" I answered.

"Yeah, right!" she responded and left us to com-plete the task.

Janet and Kathy headed into town to find some shrubs to line the front of our cabin. My sister, Gwen, was visiting that weekend and went with them. While they were gone, Becky and I spread out the brown matting and began digging in the sand to place the bullet bricks into the ground. The bricks were rounder in front and had an indented curve in back, so they fit together quite nicely.

"After you dig the hole, pull the matting into it before placing in the brick," Becky suggested. "The bricks will hold the matting in place!"

"Good idea!" I said.

We placed the brick bullets in one at a time following the line Janet had drawn for us. We used a level and made sure the tops were straight. If not, we removed or replaced sand in each hole. It was quite a deliberate process. We finished the project just as the girls got back with some beautiful shrubs. They brought them to the front as we were admiring our work.

"It looks nice, Tom," commented Janet. "Doesn't it look better than a straight line?"

"I'd have to say so, Janet."

Then, Janet leaned over and whispered in my ear. "Gwen paid for all the shrubs."

"Very generous," I whispered back with a huge grin on my face.

Steve and Jon took over from there. They cut slits in the matting, dug holes for each of the plants, and planted each shrub. When they finished, they filled the area between the plants with woods chips. As the sun was setting, we all stood and admired our landscaping in silence.

"Now, doesn't that look better?" Kathy finally asked.

The bullets really set off the edging, the brown chips around each plant looked professional, and the shrubs topped everything off. They would grow to make the front of our cabin gorgeous. Every time we look at our shrubs, we all feel a sense of pride because we did it ourselves with sweat labor!

"We'll have to do that in the backyard as well," stated Janet.

"We'll put some plants around the bunkhouse too," added Kathy.

I smiled. I appreciated the initiative the girls took because I was the one who usually took care of the lawn. Now, everyone wanted to make a contribution to make our place look attractive and beautiful. I was thrilled!

"It will take a lot of water for the roots to settle in," Steve said as he began watering the plants with the hose. "We need to water them each time we come up. Hopefully, Mother Nature will help us out too."

So, that's how many projects were accomplished. Someone had an idea, like Kathy. Someone went to work, like Jon. Once the ball got rolling, everyone seemed to jump on the bandwagon.

Once our bunkhouse was completed, it became evident that we needed to establish some boundaries as our families continued to grow. We all met and discussed some changes that needed to take place for everyone to be happy. Change does not come easily, and we needed to discuss our concerns and hammer out some guidelines.

We have decided that each family unit would have their own exclusive week from Sunday night to 4 PM on Friday during the summer. Our extended family has grown so large that it would be impossible for all of us to be together at the cabin at the same time. We have established an owners' weekend that is available only to the owners as well as an adult weekend. The rest of the weekends are open to any family that wants to come. We also have established guidelines for use of the cabin, use of the boat, filling the gas tanks before leaving, clean-up procedures, and other such matters.

We still have the cabin and love it, especially as we're getting into retirement years. It also brings us great joy to see our children and grandchildren enjoying it as much as we do. It is our hope and prayer that it will bring many more years of blessing to our family.

MY GRANDCHILDREN AT
THE CABIN

Sandy and I have fifteen grandchildren now. They all love the cabin as much as I do, and I have greatly loved watching them enjoy all the same activities that their parents did when they were young.

I asked two of my grandchildren to write some of their thoughts about this place in Wisconsin. Joseph is Katie's oldest son. He visited the cabin several times as a young boy. Starting when he was fifteen, he began to come back to Wisconsin for my family's cabin week each year. His essay is the last chapter of this book. Rachel is Mike's oldest daughter. She is a great writer. I'm including her recollections here to describe the times I have spent with my grandchildren at the cabin. Even though most of my grandchildren are older, I'm sure my brothers' families have all had or will have these same experiences with their grandchildren.

The cabin is a place where I get to play, rest, and enjoy every summer. This vacation spot offers some wonderful activities, including swimming, water skiing, fishing, and relaxing. I get to experience these things with the people I love. The cabin is a part of every summer, and it is definitely a gift from God.

I've been going to the cabin for my whole life. We go up on many weekends during the summer. On the day we leave, we pack the car and ride for a little over two hours to reach our destination. Sometimes, we stop for a meal or for ice cream on the way. I look out the window at the rows of corn, the many trees, and the Wisconsin towns. Upon arriving, I leap out of the car. The moment I hit the driveway, I hear silence. It is beautifully still. Right away, I run to the front of the cabin and see the lake. It's the first thing I always do even if I've just been there the weekend before. In the late afternoon light, the water gently laps against the sand.

The activities at the cabin vary depending on the weather, but you can enjoy yourself no matter what. Weekends at the cabin are available for anyone to come and stay. During these times, I play with my younger second cousins. Each family unit also receives their own personal week at the cabin. During our cabin week with Grandma and Grandpa, we have the cabin all to ourselves to enjoy however we wish. It is wonderful. This week is usually the best cabin experience of the year.

Our routine at the cabin is similar each day, although it varies based on weather and other factors. Here is a typical day at the cabin:

My sister wakes me up, usually around nine or ten o'clock, and informs me that breakfast will be in ten minutes. In the kitchen, Grandma is scrambling the eggs, and the table is all set and ready to go. I sit down in my usual spot, which faces the backyard. Our traditional breakfast meal includes Grandma's gooey caramel rolls and delicious eggs. If we're not having this, Grandma has almost certainly bought some sort of yummy pastry to go along with our cereal.

"Are we playing wiffleball?" I ask Dad once the meal is over.

"Yep, go get set up," he replies.

We all go outside and set up the bases in the shady backyard. The home plate is near the cabin. Sometimes, we kids just play wiffleball with Grandpa and Dad, but there have been some games where others have joined in. Grandma even stepped outside one time to bat and hit a home run.

After the game, we are ready to get wet! Quickly changing into our swimsuits, we run to the sunbathed deck in front. We get sunscreened and then wait for our sunscreen to soak in. Once it has soaked in nicely, the water sports begin.

The speedboat is a central part of our morning. After we haul the skis, kneeboard, wakeboard, and tube from the garage, our skiing time begins! Dad drives the boat all over the lake, especially in the areas he refers to as 'the flats'. These are the calmest parts of the lake that are best for water skiing.

Skiing on the lake is bliss! I jump off of the boat into the cold water and quickly pull my right foot into the ski and then the left. Then, I grab the rope and pull on it until I reach the handle. I sit in the water, bend my knees, and get both ski tips out of the water. Before long, the boat motor starts. I get pulled up amidst some spray, and then I'm flying over the water. On the calmest mornings, the lake looks like glass. Now that I am good at it, I love water skiing! The run is finished with a triumphant landing in front of our cabin.

After we finish skiing and tubing, we head back to the cabin. Soon, it is lunch time. Picnics on the deck are satisfying. We have sandwiches, cheesy chips, or hot dogs and the usual desserts of nutty bars, little cakes, or ice cream cones. We usually have a glass of soda pop as well.

After lunch, we all put on more sunscreen and go swimming again! Our spot on the lake is unique. The sandy bottom of the lake in front of the cabin is free of weeds and is fairly smooth. This makes the swimming experience better because we are not stepping on weeds or rocks. In the water, we play with floaties and the sailboard. With this board, we fool around and have balancing wars.

During the afternoon, Grandma always has a little bowl of snacks near the back door filled with treats like junior mints, peanuts, and licorice. Food at the cabin is abundant. As Grandpa says, "We eat like kings up here."

Late in the afternoon, we get dressed and walk outside to hang our wet swimsuits on the line. My bare feet tread over the dirt and dead pine needles around the clothesline. The setting sun spills down on the backyard.

"Dinner!" Mom calls from the cabin.

Our dinners are always delicious. We have hamburgers with potato salad, lasagna, chicken divan, tacos, or pizza. Dinner desserts include Grandma's strawberry shortcake (white cupcakes with strawberries and whipped cream), ice cream cones, and root beer floats.

After our delicious dinner, we ask Grandpa, "Are we going fishing tonight?"

"Sure!" he replies. "I've got the poles and tackle all ready to go."

We all get our life jackets on, grab our fishing poles, and get on the pontoon. Fishing right by the drop off in front of our cabin sometimes rewards us with a bucket full of sunnies. After a wormy, fishy experience, we head home and wash our hands. If we got a pretty good catch, Grandpa cleans them all up so we can enjoy them later.

Now, it's time for a campfire. The firewood is lit up, and the singing begins! Grandpa sings all of the classics from memory while we adjust the burning logs with the metal poker and roast marshmallows over the fire. The music is part of the campfire tradition. I often play songs as well. These campfires also include storytelling and joking. Sometimes in July, we have fireworks as well.

Soon, the stars come out overhead. As the fire burns low, I head out on the dock and sit down on the bench. Frogs chirp to each other in the dark. Our full day is drawing to a close. We head inside where the living room is quiet now. Grandma sits in her spot on the couch talking to Mom. I head into the bathroom, brush my teeth, and climb into my bed. Tomorrow will hold more cabin activities.

When I was younger, my cabin experience was slightly different than it is now. We played a lot more in the yard and on the beach. A large pine tree stands in the front yard of the cabin. A few years ago, my siblings and I turned the area underneath the branches into a fort. Amy made a makeshift broom of sticks, swept dead pine needles, and made beds and cushions. Ryan used a string to hook a branch in such a way that it was a door. The lake was higher then, and we used an empty water bottle to draw water from the lake. Sap clung to the nearby trees. I was especially fascinated with this 'glue' and glued all sorts of things together with a sap stick. Dad insisted that we couldn't use this fort in the early summer during tick season. The lower branches have since been trimmed from this pine tree, so the fort ceases to exist. It was great fun for us when we had it though.

When I was only seven years old, I began to learn how to water ski. I was scared and remember one particular night when I did not want to try again the next day. But, I did. However, I would get cold, and my parents would make "deals" with me, like "five more tries". I didn't totally get the hang of it that summer, but the next summer I kept trying. Soon, I was able to go in a circle around the lake. My water-skiing abilities continued to grow. There was a time when I was working on standing up straight. Later, I went in and out of the wake, although I didn't get comfortable with this for quite awhile. I learned to let go of the rope with one hand and wave. Eventually, I began working on dropping a ski. While I did try this a handful of times, I didn't get the hang of it. Then, I tried getting up on one ski and was successful. Now, I love to water ski. I am good at it and enjoy going in and out of the wake. The best days to ski are when the lake is relatively calm all over with certain spots as smooth as glass. I am glad that I get to participate in this sport every summer!

We often played Dark Tag, a nighttime game, when we were younger. While the adults sat around the campfire, we kids would sneak off to hide in the bushes and chase each other in the dark. Once when we were playing, my cousin, Joseph, was hiding on one of the hills in the backyard. He jumped to his feet to run away and tripped on a metal stake sticking in the ground. His jeans got a large tear down one side. That was the end of that game.

The cabin is a place where I can enjoy summer activities with my family in a restful, relaxing environment. We laugh around the dinner table, play card games in the living room, and sit around the campfire enjoying others' goofiness. I have many special summer memories of swimming in the sparkling lake, walking barefoot across the lawn, flying across the water behind the boat, and getting warm in the sun while reading my book. I treasure the special moments I have enjoyed sitting on the dock below the canopy of stars and walking on the edge of the gently lapping lake with my bare feet treading on the sand.

The cabin and the summer activities it holds have been a great blessing of my childhood. Thank you, Lord, for the cabin.

Rachel Hall

It has really blessed me to see Mike and his family enjoying the cabin, and I enjoy having them live close to me.

During the summer of 2013, Sandy and I flew out to Washington to celebrate our fiftieth wedding anniversary with Katie. Mike and his family also drove out there. After the celebration, Katie's four oldest daughters, Haley, Olivia, Grace, and Victoria, flew back with us to spend a few days at our cabin. This was a special trip for them because my granddaughters hadn't been back in many years. Becky, Ryan, Rachel, and Amy would join us, and Mike would come up on the weekend.

The girls stayed a few days with their other grandparents. I went up to our cabin for a golf tournament that we help host each year. About forty guys, including my brothers, Jon and Steve, and nephews, Doug and Scott, come up for this big event. The guys stay at one of four cabins in the area including ours. The tournament lasts for three days, and we play a total of seventy-two holes of golf at various courses. It is a real blast. The cabin has blessed a lot of people thanks to this golf tournament.

When the last golfer had left, I cleaned up the cabin as best I could. I sat relaxing on the deck waiting for my family to arrive. Suddenly, I heard the sound of joyful screaming as the girls ran toward the front of the cabin. They came charging around the side of the cabin and scrambled up the deck to give me a hug. I immediately observed the excitement and joy which radiated from their faces.

"Victoria, are you dreaming or are you really here?" I asked.

"Oh, Grandpa!" responded Tori as she pinched herself. "I'm really here with you at the cabin. We're going to have a blast!"

Just then, Becky came on the deck. She gave me a hug and then turned to the girls.

"We won't go swimming just yet," she said. "We have to get settled in our rooms and help Grandma with everything."

After everything was unloaded and organized, Becky finally told the girls they could go swimming. The girls rushed into their rooms to put on their swim suits. Then, they all ran down to the dock, held hands, and ran off the end of the dock. The cool, spring fed water immersed them completely. They came up out of the water screaming with delight.

"Finally, I'm here after five years," Grace screamed. "I am so happy!"

After a marvelous one hour swim, they all climbed out of the lake, strolled into the cabin, and changed into their clothes. They played games until dinner was ready. That night, we enjoyed a delicious meal of sloppy joes. As I looked around our huge wooden table, I saw six of my granddaughters all smiling and laughing. It was just the beginning of a great time together.

The next morning after a delicious breakfast, everyone got on their swimsuits and jumped into the lake. Ryan, Rachel, and Amy skied first to give Katie's girls a picture of good water skiing while I drove the boat. They made it look easy, but they had grown up skiing. Their cousins were just beginning, and it was a lot harder for them. As I watched them try again and again, I remembered how hard it was for my own children when they were learning to ski. Everyone was determined, but no one was successful that morning. We did enjoy some fun tube rides though.

After a fun afternoon, delicious dinner, and pontoon ride around the lake, we started up a campfire in the firepit. The waves were gently lapping against the shore making a smooth, rhythmic sound. Of course, we roasted marshmallows and made s'mores. Then, we got out our guitars and ukulele and began singing together. The fire began to burn down into beautiful glowing coals.

We were surprised when my niece Mandy, Steve's daughter, her husband Jared, and Lonnie and Dar,

Jared's parents, appeared. A few years earlier, Steve and his children had purchased a cabin on the lake just up the road from ours. They were all staying there.

"Hi, Jared, how are you?" I said greeting him with a handshake.

"We're doing great, Tom," he responded.

"Grab a chair and join us," I stated.

The fun continued as we talked, laughed, and told stories. The night moved in and the bright stars filled the dark black sky. I couldn't be happier.

"Girls, would you mind singing a few songs for Jared's parents?" I asked.

"We would love to," responded Haley.

The six girls stood up together while the rest of us watched from our chairs around the campfire. Grace played the guitar. They all looked so young and beautiful with the glow of the fire reflecting on their faces. Their first song was "Grandpa", one of my favorites. I watched Lonnie and Dar's faces as the girls began to sing. As the song continued, tears slowly emerged on Lonnie's face with Dar looking on in amazement. The six girls sang with their smooth sweet voices in harmony. It's hard to capture the feeling during that evening with words, but I will never forget that moment. It was sacred.

The rest of our time was as wonderful as that first day. My granddaughters continued to enjoy the cabin with everything they had. Kari, Steve's other daughter, came up to their cabin with her twins, and the girls enjoyed playing with them and blessing them. Olivia, Grace, and Victoria were able to go a short distance on skis. We decided to get the kneeboard out, and that worked much better. We enjoyed a wonderful swim in the middle of the lake and some good fishing. When Mike came up to join us, we got the sailboat out. Everyone had a turn cruising across the lake and back with Mike. At the end of the last swim, the girls all held hands and shared their favorite cabin memories while Becky videoed them. Before we left, they all stood on the shore waving good-bye to one of the most wonderful places on earth.

I have many special memories of this time and of many other times like it from years past. I couldn't record them all if I wanted to. I am so grateful to God for giving me a close family and a place that Sandy and I can share with our grandkids. I look forward to seeing how the cabin holds our family together in the future.

A TIME OF REFLECTION

One Saturday morning, I arose from bed early. All the families were at the cabin. I was tired after a late Friday evening game of cards, treats, and stimulating dialogue. Sandy, as usual, managed to get up before me and put on a pot of coffee. I jumped out of bed, snuck into the bathroom, shaved, brushed my teeth, and took a quick shower as quietly as possible. Afterwards, I wandered into the living room wearing shorts, a tee shirt, and a baseball cap. Sandy was sitting on the couch sipping a hot cup of coffee.

"Good morning, Sandy. Did you sleep well?"

"As a matter of fact, I did," she responded as she gazed at me above her glasses.

She was reading her devotional book, and I did not want to interrupt her quiet time.

"I'll just grab a cup of coffee and head on out to the dock."

We had purchased a new aluminum roll out dock. Our twenty year old steel dock had seen better days, so we replaced it. Our new dock had an L-shaped section with a bench on the end. It was my favorite place to sit early in the morning while I drank my hot coffee. I filled up a cup with the fresh brew in the kitchen, maneuvered through the living room, and crept down the deck stairs heading for my favorite spot in the world.

As I strolled toward the lake, I observed a tiny hummingbird drinking nectar from a flower in our neighbor's garden. Going on a little further, I saw a woodpecker making uniform holes in our birch tree. I ambled down our makeshift railroad tie stairs and onto our dock.

The sun shone brightly on the eastern horizon. The sky was beautiful with its soft blue color, and the crystal clear waters of North Sand Lake sparkled in the sunlight. My senses were filled with delight. I sat on the bench with my hands clutched around my coffee cup and inhaled deeply. My lungs filled with pure oxygen.

"It doesn't get any better than this," I said out loud as my eyes scanned the blue waters of our lake.

As I sat in silence on the bench gazing at the water below me, my eyes brightened. A huge bass was swimming slowly below searching for minnows. I set my coffee cup into the cup holder on the arm of the bench and scurried back to the cabin. I grabbed my fishing rod which already had an orange rapala attached to the end of the line. When I reached the end of the dock, my eyes searched the clear waters for any sign of the huge bass. Suddenly, I spotted the fish swimming toward the shoreline, and my heart began to race. I cast my line into the water just ahead of the fish. It spotted the bait, turned toward it, and then swam away. I quickly reeled in my line and sent another cast right in front of the fish. This time, the monster turned quickly and grabbed my bait. I made a quick jerk with my rod to set the hook firmly in the fish's mouth. My rod began jerking and bending as the bass began its fight.

I had the drag set. The fish was swimming hard toward deeper water. I knew I could never get this huge fish up on the dock without a net, so I began walking back toward shore playing the fish as best I could. When I reached the shoreline, I continue my battle. The fish was struggling for freedom. It thrashed and pulled on my line which, thankfully, held. As the fish was tiring, I reeled harder to bring it closer toward shore. As the fish was approaching me, it suddenly broke water and jumped about two feet in the air. Shaking its head, it tried to release the hook from its mouth.

After a few more minutes, I had the bass flopping on the shore. I grabbed it under its mouth, removed the hook, and headed back toward the cabin with the prize in my hand. It was extremely heavy and maybe weighed about five pounds. Clearly, it was the biggest bass that I had ever caught!

When I reached the door of our cabin, I opened it with my left hand while holding the bass in my right hand.

"Sandy, you've got to see this!"

She came to the door. When she saw it, she couldn't believe her eyes.

"Wow! That's the biggest fish I've ever seen."

"Yeah, and it put up a tremendous fight! I had to beach it because I could never have gotten it on the dock. It would have snapped my line."

"What are you going to do with it, Tom?"

"I'm going to release it. Is anyone else up yet?"

"No, everyone is sleeping in."

"Too bad. I wanted Jon to see this one. I'm putting it back in the water because I don't want it to die. It fought so hard that it deserves to live," I explained.

I headed back to the lake. When I reached the shore, I held my bass with two hands and gently placed it in the water.

"Thanks for the memory, big fellow. Have a good life," I stated out loud.

The bass swished its tail and darted off into freedom. I returned my fishing rod to my room, refilled my coffee cup, and returned to the bench on the dock thrilled about my recent adventure. As I was sitting lost in the moment, I heard footsteps coming toward me on the dock. I turned to see Jon approaching.

"Sandy tried to tell me you caught a monster."

"You wouldn't believe it, Jon. I threw the rapala just over its head. It grabbed it, and the fight was on."

"Let's see the fish, Tommy."

"I released it."

"Why didn't you clean it? It would have made a great meal."

"I couldn't, Jon. It fought so hard that it deserved to be set free. I know you're the fisherman in the family, but you have never caught a bass that size!"

Just then, Steve and Bob walked toward us with coffee cups in hand. After I retold the fish story, we just sat in silence for a while. Finally, Bob broke the silence.

"You guys can't even begin to imagine what this place does for me after spending a year in the Bronx," he said.

Bob is a pastor and lives in the Bronx of New York City. He has been there for over forty years.

"What do you mean, Bob?" questioned Steve.

"I live in a crowded city in a tough section of the Bronx," he said. "Jeannie and I love it there because that is our home. It's where we've been called to serve. Even so, it is stressful at times. Coming back here to this beautiful spot releases the stress and brings me back again. It's hard to explain, but I don't think I could carry on if I didn't have this place to look forward to."

"It's amazing to me that the Hall boys, who didn't have a pot to pee in, own this place together," responded Jon.

"Remember when we were here as young boys on the other lot?" I asked. "We were building our boathouse that Dave insisted on having. After a day's work, we went to the point and swam just off of the deep drop off."

"Yeah!" said Steve. "The water was crystal clear. We walked out into the water about twenty feet, and the lake bottom dropped straight down to….I don't know how far. It was so beautiful underwater. I remember seeing air bubbles around us, and there were absolutely no weeds anywhere."

"At that time, there were very few people around. It seemed like we owned the whole peninsula," threw in Jon.

"I'm sorry Dave never got to see our new cabin. He would have been thrilled," I stated.

"We really owe him big time. This place is his dream. He thought outside the box, and just look at the result!" included Bob.

"You know, Dad was taken from us a young age," I said. "I struggled and felt cheated losing my father. We had some tough times growing up. Mom served us as best she could, but we really didn't appreciate it or help much. I just wish Dad could have been alive to see this place and meet his great grandkids," I commented.

"You know, if we lost this place tomorrow, I would still be grateful for all it has done for our families and children," stated Bob.

"It's like God has taken care of us as a family!" exclaimed Jon with passion. "Mom and Dad loved the Lord. They raised us to be Christians and were examples before us. They, as well as Dave, are in heaven. We will see them again and be able to tell them our story. Maybe they already know it and are pulling for us."

Jon looked at all of us.

"We are blessed men!" he said. "We have godly wives, wonderful children and grandchildren, and this great place to come to together. Maybe we take this place for granted sometimes. But, when you think of where we've come from, I would have to say it's a God thing. This cabin is totally a miracle that has been given to our extended family,

"Wow! Well said, little brother!" I chuckled.

We must have sat on that dock for hours and reminisced. We broke into singing old songs, told stories, laughed, and at times shed tears. I am so fortunate to be in the family I am in. I love being a part of a large family. We have learned to love, support, encourage, and help one another. The cabin has played a huge part in that.

The story is not over. We brothers still have each other and this wonderful cabin. It is as close to heaven on earth as I can imagine. It is my hope and prayer that this place will keep us together as we grow older and watch our grandkids grow to adulthood. I can't tell you how much I love this place and how grateful I am for this great gift from our Lord to the Hall family.

SURROUNDED BY LOVE

by Joseph Pates

A soft gray light streams through the slightly open window. I roll over in bed and look at the ceiling of the bunkhouse. Shaking the sleep from my eyes, I glance at the clock. It reads quarter to five. The night is old.

"Too early," I think to myself.

I roll over and stare at the wall, closing my eyes. Then, I remember that the sun will be rising soon. Quietly, I get out of bed and pull on some clothes. Slipping a baseball cap on my head, I silently leave my room as to not disturb the others still in slumberland. The screen door squeaks on its hinges as it scrapes across the doormat. I head for the garage. In the old fridge, I find a container of baby nightcrawlers.

The dew drenches my feet as I head across the lawn. The air is fresh and pure and smells of wet grass, dew, and pine. My bare feet tread on the carpet of sandy brown pine needles as I head around the corner to the front of the cabin. I grab a fishing pole from the corner of the deck, stroll back down the weathered cedar steps, and head for the bench on the end of the dock. I walk past the hammock, down the railroad tie steps, and pass by the pontoon and speedboat. Hooking a baby nightcrawler securely on my line, I cast it out into the water and sit down on the bench.

North Sand Lake is as calm as a sheet of glass, and the morning air is still and cool. A few puffy clouds glide across the eastern horizon, where an ominous glow of orange is beginning to form. I set my pole down and pick up my camera in anticipation.

The orange haze gradually gets brighter, and then a ray of light breaks out from behind the eastern horizon. A loon calls from out on the lake, its warbling giggle greeting the morning with joy and laughter. A second ray comes out and then a third. Finally, a globe of solid orange quietly emerges from behind the opposite shoreline. The light it casts out sets the clouds on fire and contrasts with the deeper blue of the sky. The words of the Psalmist cross my mind, "From the rising of the sun to the going down of the same, the name of the Lord shall be praised."

I turn around and look back towards the cabin. It shines in the radiance of the morning glory with each window catching the rays of the sun and selflessly reflecting it back towards me. The stately pine, spruce, maple, and ash glow with a deep green, the color of life. The sandy brown siding has never looked so good. I see the inner tubes and noodles leaning against the left side of the cabin. Their rest will soon be over.

Shifting on the bench, I snap a few pictures and then pick up my pole again. After about an hour, I quietly mosey off the dock and head back to the bunkhouse with about ten beautiful pictures on my stringer and no fish. But, the morning had just begun.

After another hour of sleep, I dress again, spend a few moments with my Bible, and head across the lawn towards the cabin. Pulling the back door open, I walk into the cabin, leave my shoes on the mat, and greet Grandma and Becky as they bustle around the kitchen preparing breakfast. The smell of coffee and caramel rolls fills the air. I head out the front door and sit on the deck with Grandpa. We admire the panoramic view before us as we talk together in sweet mutual fellowship. Out on the lake, a jet ski tears across the surface of the water which the morning breeze is now stirring and moving.

I am so happy to be alive. I feel the joy of the jet skier as he spins around and shouts with exhilaration. The birds sing from the nearby trees, each one blending its own song into a beautiful symphony of perfect harmony. The hum of a trolling motor reaches my ears, and I imagine a contented fisherman calmly smoking his pipe and eagerly watching his pole for any action.

It is breakfast time. I sit down at the huge well-worn table, lovingly used by four generations of Halls and still going strong. As Grandpa prays the blessing, I look up at the painting on the wall and observe the old Swedish man bending over his humble meal of gruel. His hands are folded in prayer. I bow my own head. As I heartily dig into the sweet caramel rolls, crisp fruit, and warm scrambled eggs, I think again about how much I have to be thankful for.

After bringing my plate and cup to the sink, I head over to the bunkhouse and pull on my swimsuit. Back on the cabin deck, I apply a generous amount of sunscreen, so I will not have any regrets when I am Grandpa's age. After climbing into the paddleboat, I head out onto the lake. Drifting out many yards from shore, I dangle my feet in the water and lean back to allow the sun's rays to kiss my face. This is serendipity at its best.

Then, I hear the sound of the ski boat and watch as it speeds off across the lake with one of my cousins tightly gripping the handle of the rope. I slowly paddle back to the dock, tie up the paddleboat, and jump off the end of the dock into the refreshingly cool water. I pull the water skis off of the dock and slip them onto my feet. The boat comes sailing back in. Ryan lets go of the rope and comes gliding smoothly across the water. With arms held high in the air, he sinks slowly down into the water. I catch the handle of the ski rope, and lift the tips of my skis out of the water.

"Hit it!"

The engine roars. I bend my knees and lean back and effortlessly pop up out of the water. I shake the water out of my eyes. With my arms locked firmly into position and my knees bent, I sail across the lake. As I fly along behind the boat, I think about previous times at the cabin, about the many times I had tried to ski and failed, about my persistence and perseverance, and about the day I had finally gotten up. I smile as I think about the confidence I now have as a result of learning to ski.

Mike is driving the boat to a calmer section of the lake. As we round the point, I see the flats, the clear mass unbroken by waves and as smooth as butter, calling my name. Leaning out, I effortlessly slip into the calm outside the wake of the humming motor. I enjoy the feel of the glassy sheet of water before re-entering the wake with a burst of spray. We loop in a big circle and head back for the cabin. I head out of the wake a second time and let go of the rope. Gradually, I sink down into the water for a perfect landing. After pulling my skis off, I hand them to Rachel and climb into the boat to watch the joy of others.

When all are done skiing and the boat is secured in the shore station, we all pull off our life jackets and jump off the dock into the lake. The spring fed water is crystal clear and refreshing. I float on my back, feeling the cool embrace of the lake. We all laugh as we splash each other, and the cannonballs get bigger and bigger.

After we finish our hearty lunch, we head to the backyard to play a round of badminton. The air is warming fast. After a hard-fought round, we all put on our life jackets and climb onto the pontoon. The old motor sputters and fumes, and the distinctive odor of gasoline fills the air. We glide slowly out to the middle of the lake talking, laughing, and teasing each other. Once we have reached just the right spot, Grandpa shuts off the motor. The time has come for a deep lake swim.

One of my cousins and I grab my little brother by his feet and hands and throw him into the water. I dive off of the front of the pontoon, my hands pointed in front of me, and feel the cool water envelop my face and body. One by one, we all continuously circle around the pontoon by climbing up the ladder, running across the pontoon, and jumping into the lake with a tremendous splash. This is the definition of refreshing.

When we return to the cabin, I sit in a lawn chair by the fire pit peeling a stick of white pine. The blade of my knife penetrates the bark and sends it rolling off of the stick in little curly shavings. The sharp, wonderful smell of pine sap covers my hands. I think of the walking sticks that line the wall of my bedroom back home. Each one is a precious memory of time spent at the cabin.

Everyone is relaxing. Grandpa is lounging in the hammock slowly swinging back and forth. Becky is sitting on the beach, reading her book, and enjoying every minute of her vacation. Amy, as always, is splashing in the water off the dock. My brother, Jesse, is building a sand castle on the beach. Rachel is drying off on the deck, and Ryan is sitting near me. We talk and crack jokes as I work on my stick. Grandma is inside, sitting in her place on the couch, mending some article of clothing she has brought up. Mike is hidden away in his room in the bunkhouse taking his afternoon nap. All are content. Life is good.

Later that evening, we all gather around the table again. Becky has prepared a delicious meal for us. As we eat our dinner, starving from all of the day's activities, we revel and rejoice in fellowship with each other as we talk and laugh. The Lord has truly blessed our family with unity, peace, and love. For that, I am grateful.

We head back out onto the pontoon armed with our tackle boxes and fishing poles after dinner. The motor roars, and we charge out into the calm evening looking to have a good night of fishing. Motoring down to a tried and true fishing hole, we begin to cast and reel in our lines. Our hooks are set with plump, juicy worms. We catch many sunfish worth keeping and throw the little ones back in for another day. My little brother pulls in a bass about fourteen inches long. I see the joy on his face as he holds up his trophy. The way he is smiling, you'd think he had just pulled in a forty-four inch northern pike.

As we idly watch our bobbers, the sun begins to gradually descend below the western horizon. Its dying light illuminates the clouds. Their light effervescently reflects on the calm water of the lake. The air is still in calm, and I hear the night noises beginning to emerge from the forest.

Upon returning to our cabin, Grandpa filets the fish and brings them inside to the freezer. Rachel heads into the cabin and returns with two guitars. I drop my load of kindling and firewood and build a fire in the firepit, tenderly setting each piece in just the right place. Amy and Ryan set up the chairs, and Mike lights up the firewood teepee of birch and pine that I have just built. It incinerates instantly, and its bright orange light quickly outshines the fading light of the setting sun. The crackle of the burning logs pierces the evening, and a column of wood smoke ascends toward the sky, filling the air with its acid smell. Night has descended.

Tuning up our guitars, we begin to sing the same old songs that have been sung around this same firepit for over thirty years. We laugh at the same old jokes and tell the same old stories. In this, we are one with the decades. We are sharing in the joy that has permeated the atmosphere of this campfire for many years past. Lord willing, that same joy and mutual fellowship will surround these ash-blackened stones for decades to come.

Someone brings out a bag of marshmallows, chocolate, and graham crackers. After my second s'more, I pick up a guitar. The high, sweet sound of my harmonica blends with the chirping of the crickets and the humming of the mosquitoes. I begin to sing a song I had written. It was the fruit of a late night of anticipation and written in expectancy of a day like I had just experienced.

There's a beautiful spot in the state of Wisconsin
Just a hundred miles north of Eau Claire.
Drive through Burnett County and make your turn at Webster
And pretty soon you will be there.
Nestled there on Sand Lake is a beautiful cabin
That's owned by the brothers called Hall.
There we have fun and spend time as a family
This place is well loved by us all.
It's the little brown cabin on the clear blue lake
Where the deep green trees stretch so tall.
I'm headed on my way to the little brown cabin
That's owned by the brothers called Hall.
We ski in the morning and we fish in the evening
And we swim in the lake in the afternoon.
We sit on the deck in the cool of the daytime
And listen to the call of the loon.
We sit around the campfire and talk and laugh together
Someone plays guitar and we all sing.
And then it's not long before everyone is sleeping
As the night noises through the forest ring.
Oh, life is so good in the woods of Wisconsin
At the little brown cabin on the lake.
Surrounded by God's love and the love of our family
A better experience you couldn't make.
It's the little brown cabin on the clear blue lake
Where the deep green trees stretch so tall
I'm headed on my way to the little brown cabin
That's owned by the brothers called Hall.

While the others head inside to hit the hay, I remain by the fire alone. Laying down my guitar, I lean forward in my chair. The fire has burned down to coals. I can feel the heat radiating from the glowing embers and smell the pine sap burning in the few logs that remain in the firepit. The sounds of the North Woods close in around me, and the night has now descended upon this place.

I think again of the words that I wrote:

Surrounded by God's love and the love of our family
A better experience you couldn't make.

Indeed, on this side of eternity, it would be hard to top this day that I had enjoyed. I sit back in my chair and begin to think.

I am surrounded, totally surrounded, by love. I feel the love of God pressing near to my heart. This place has been dedicated to Him, and He has blessed it, Whenever I am there, I feel close to Him. I bow my head for a moment and pray that my home someday will have this same effect on whoever comes into it.

I am also surrounded by the love of my family. I can feel the love of Grandma and Becky, sacrificially giving of their time and energy to feed me delicious meals and clean up after all of us. I can feel the love of each of my cousins whom I have grown closer to as a result of our time here together. I can feel the love of my brother and am grateful that I brought him with me to share this experience.

I feel the love of my great-uncle Dave. I look around me and see the fruits of the vision that he had. I think about his love for this place, his love for his family, and about the role of leadership he had played. I feel a special closeness to him and eagerly anticipate the day I will meet him in heaven. I think of the hard work of my grandpa and all of his brothers. Their nickels, dimes, quarters, and long hours of labor provided the funds necessary to buy this land my feet are resting on and to build the cabin I come to each summer. I am filled with gratitude to them and to their wives for their dedication, sacrifice, and generous gift to me.

Most of all, I feel the love of my grandpa whose book you are currently holding in your hands. I think about how he keeps the vision going by imparting it to the next generation. I think about how blessed I am to call Grandpa one of my closest friends. I think about everything that he has taught me. I think about how he surrendered his life to Jesus that night lying on his back lawn, and the impact he has made on the world since that day. I think about how we share many of the same interests and passions, so many of which lie up at this special place in Wisconsin. As the wood smoke curls upward into the night sky, I think about how much he loves this place. I think about what it will be like to come up to this place when he is gone. I know it will be different. I wonder if the second and third generation will take the torch and pass on the vision by preserving the same spirit of joy, fellowship, grace, unity, and love that fills this special spot. But, that belongs to the future. I am alive today.

As I sit in front of the fire, now nearing the end of its life, I breathe a prayer of gratitude to God for the wonderful gift He gave me in the cabin. I give thanks for this season in my life when I can come to this place, take my foot off of the accelerator, and relax. I pray that I will be able to re-enter the life I left behind rejuvenated and refreshed from the day I had just experienced and the several days to come.

After putting out the fire, I walk out to the end of the dock. The bugs have all gone away, and not a sound breaks the silence. The lake is still and quiet. I take one final breath of the night air and walk back to the bunkhouse.

I roll up in my blanket on the bed and fall asleep instantly, surrounded and filled to overflowing by love: the love of God, the love of my family, the love of my grandpa, and the love of the cabin.

Joseph Pates

SUNRISE ON SAND LAKE

Roused by peering eyes of gray ghostly shadows and
leaning feathery columns
surrendering gossamer form to looming dawn.
An eerie stillness cast over a sea of darkened glass
commands reverential silence
while eastern edge unfurls its golden banner
setting boundaries of azur and honey.
A noisome loon dares harmonize with air and water
protesting rightful ownership,
challenging trespassers o'er its aquatic domain.
The banner lifts and casts its store of diamonds across the
watery plain.
They dance to rhythms of wave and wind,
Accompanied by the voice of the prophet ever singing:
Day after day they pour forth speech;
Night after night they display knowledge.

-Robert Glenn ("Bob") Hall
2009